D1649526

EDINBURGH CHARACTERS

MICHAEL
T R B TURNBULL

SAINT ANDREW PRESS
1992

Book Fair 1995

Published by
SAINT ANDREW PRESS
121 George Street, Edinburgh EH2 4YN

Copyright © Michael T R B Turnbull 1992

ISBN 0 7152 0671 0

British Library Cataloguing in Publication Data
A catalogue record for this book
is available from the British Library

ISBN 0715206710

Design concept by Mark Blackadder.
Illustrations on pages 3, 8, 14, 34(x2), 37, 42, 43, 48, 49,
53, 56, 57, 61, 63, 68, 76, 79, 80, 96, 97, 106, 112, 117,
125, 126, 128, 129, 133, 135, 140, 141, 142 and 146 by
Michael T R B Turnbull.
Etchings on pages iv, viii, 2, 4, 13, 19, 21, 27, 31, 46, 72,
93, 99, 113, 119, 120, 122 and 153 from Cassell's *Old and
New Edinburgh* in 3 volumes, James Grant (1887); and on
page 41 from *Literary Landmarks of Edinburgh*, Laurence
Hutton, 1891.
Cover photograph of author by David F Turner.
Typeset in 11.5/14 pt Garamond.
Printed and **bound** by Athenaeum Press Ltd, Newcastle
upon Tyne.

CONTENTS

The LAWNMARKET *with* ST GILES *in the* BACKGROUND 1825

EDINBURGH

The CHARACTER *of a* CITY

In the waist of Scotland, where the Forth river swells into the open sea, lies the city of Edinburgh, born out of one of the many volcanic crags in which the eastern tracts of the Lothians abound. From the stronghold of the rock, 440 feet above sea-level, a determined garrison could successfully dominate the approach by land or water. Few traces of early occupation remain, for the oldest building still standing in the city is Queen Margaret's Chapel, constructed around 1090 on what is now the Castle Rock.

The ground slopes away from Edinburgh Castle in a mile-long 'crag and tail' ridge towards the east, and it was along the spine of this ridge (now the Royal Mile) that the ancient burgh grew in the protection of the castle, defended to the north by the deep water of the Nor' Loch. In this small medieval city the burghers kept their crofts, a handful of cattle, pigs or sheep, and wrestled a precarious living out of the soil.

With the founding of Holyrood abbey in 1128 and St Giles parish kirk (1130), Edinburgh followed the traditional medieval pattern of Castle, Burgh and Abbey. After the Battle of Flodden in 1513, when the burgh was nearly destroyed, a strong defensive wall was constructed to replace the earlier King's Wall. For the next 200 years the Flodden Wall marked the boundaries of the Old Town.

There were now four main points of entry to the burgh—the Netherbow Port (gate), the Cowgate Port, Bristo Port and the West Port. Below, to the east, at the foot of the ridge, lay the new burgh of Canongate, granted by the King to the Augustinian canons in the Abbey of Holy-rood. Until 1690 the Canongate remained an independent burgh, then Edinburgh bought it over.

Until around 1550 most High Street houses were constructed on a timber frame-work with brightly coloured plaster or clay infilling; the roofs were thatch or slate.

After 1550 the danger of fire led to more houses being built of locally quarried stone, roofed with red clay pantiles. With so many people wanting to live inside the protection of the Flodden Wall, storeys were piled one on top of another, up to as many as nine, producing the characteristic 'lands' (medieval tower-blocks). In one instance behind Parliament Square (now demolished), there were 14 storeys. Some say that seventeenth century Edinburgh, not New York, invented the skyscraper.

Often the gable-ends were built to face the street, and 'closes' (blind alleys) or 'wynds' (open alleys) were needed to allow access to the front doors or to the 'courts' (courtyards). Sometimes a close was framed by an arch wide enough to allow a cart through—this was known as a 'pend.'

Merchants conducted daily business below the Mercat (market) Cross in the centre of the High Street until 1753, when the Royal Exchange (later known as the City Chambers) was built. Proclamations were also made at the Mercat Cross.

At first burghs were the only place where trade and commerce could be carried on in accordance with Royal Charter. This enabled the King to maintain close control over trade and to collect taxes regularly.

There were specific selling-points for other commodities: a weekly grain and live-stock market held in the Grassmarket; a wool and linen sale held once a week in the part of the High Street known as the Land or Lawn Market. Other necessities such as meat or butter were purchased in special walled markets. As the town spread, so did the places of commerce and trade.

Next to the kirk of St Giles in the High Street was the Old Tolbooth which served as a meeting-place for the Town Council, the Burgh Council, supreme courts and even the Scottish Parliament, and it served as the central tax collection office. The virtue of the Tolbooth was that it was secure, and this explains its notoriety as the town jail.

The Old Tolbooth was demolished in 1817.

Further down the High Street at the Tron stood the weigh-beam where that indispensable commodity, salt, was measured and sold. Throughout the burgh a number of wells quenched the burgh's thirst and provided the citizens with water to wash in.

The ruling body of the town, from medieval times until 1832, was the Town or Burgh Council, composed of merchants and members of the exclusive craft guilds. By 1600 there were 14 incorporated trades.

Below them in the social scale came the journeymen, servants, labourers and the beggars, the 'outland' folk from outside the burgh, the 'unfreemen,' the vagabonds and gypsies.

Skilled trades such as baking, butchering, shoemaking, goldsmithing or tailoring were exclusively in the hands of the guilds and the merchants. Whereas the guilds were permitted to manufacture the finer articles, only the merchants could conduct trade on an international basis.

The Luckenbooths (permanent enclosed shops built up against St Giles) housed the goldsmiths,

CITY *of* EDINBURGH
COAT *of* ARMS
(NINETEENTH CENTURY)

jewellers, watchmakers and booksellers until after the Reformation, but by 1830 this permanent structure was done away with and the booths sold only cheap toys, sweets, shoes or second-hand clothes.

The Krames (open stalls erected against the buttresses of St Giles) were used by the unfreemen to sell their goods on market days, the only occasions on which they could lawfully do so in the early history of the burgh.

Between 1790 and 1830 the draining of the Nor' Loch and the construction of two bridges and an earthen Mound linking the High Street with Princes Street, accelerated the development of the New Town to the north of the Old. The Treaty of Union between England and Scotland in 1707 signalled the end of the Old Town's siege mentality and its community spirit, and heralded the arrival of a more leisurely and cosmopolitan style of living.

Like Topsy, the Old Town 'just grew' in an exciting and often chaotic huddle. The New Town, however, was based on the logical grid-iron design of the 23 year old architect James Craig, who in 1766 won the competition organised by the Town Council. Craig's design was an orderly and severely geometric one, freed from the constraints imposed on the Old Town architecture by the slope of the High Street and by the confines of the Flodden Wall.

Further development of the New Town by the architects Robert Adam and William Playfair added to the classical elegance and dignity of the site with spacious terraces and stately columns, but what perhaps got lost along the way was the Old Town's lively 'democracy of the common stair.'

The maintenance of law and order in the city had at first been the duty of the burghers ('watching and warding'). In 1689 a Town Guard was established which quickly gained a reputation for cowardice, incompetence and cursing, which earned its members the scornful nickname of 'The Town Rats.' During the execution of a criminal in 1736 the Guard panicked and fired into the crowd. The disturbances which followed were later known as the Porteous Riots after the trigger-happy officer in command.

Later the Clearances drove Highlanders in large numbers into the Lowland towns to look for work. The Industrial Revolution at the same time forced many agricultural workers from all parts of the country into the same towns. Both factors increased overcrowding, insanitation and the poverty of many in cities such as Edinburgh. As the New Town was built, the gentry moved out of the Old Town, leaving it to decay into tenement slums crammed with poorly paid labourers, artisans and the destitute. Robert Louis Stevenson, writing of the Old

Town as he knew it in the 1870s, gives a striking picture of its degeneration and misery: 'In one house, perhaps, two score families herd together, and, perhaps, not one of them is wholly out of the reach of want. The great hotel is given over to discomfort from the foundation to chimney-tops, everywhere a pinching, narrow habit, scanty meals, and an air of sluttishness and dirt. In the first room there is a birth, in another a death, in a third a sordid drinking-bout .... Social inequality is nowhere more ostentatious that at Edinburgh ....'

Between 1770 and 1800 the population of Edinburgh doubled to 80,000 and continued to rise meteorically until the end of the nineteenth century. Crimes of a minor variety increased and the Town Guard, and later the police force, were kept busy. In 1847, for example, there were 176 known housebreakings, 257 cases of carters riding furiously, 1472 cases of begging and 5573 persons found drunk in the streets.

Gradually the traditional diet of oatmeal gave way to imported wheat, poor in minerals and vitamins. The low wage earner in the town received an inadequate supply of fresh fruit, vegetables and milk. The high tenements cut off sunlight, and the pall of smoke over the city absorbed the ultra-violet rays. Rickets and tuberculosis became the scourge of the labouring poor.

Until the end of the eighteenth century

there was no organised cleansing of the town. At 10 o' clock every night in the Old Town, a drum sounded and housewives in the tenements shouted 'Gardyloo!' (*Gardez l'eau* or *Garde à l'eau*—Watch out for the water!) as they threw slops and waste down into the street below, adding to the piles of decaying rubbish. Imagine the stink. It was known at home and abroad as 'Edina's Roses' (or *Flou'rs o' Edinbro*).

The New Town also had its share of embarrassment, like the failure of the National Monument on Calton Hill, over-looking Princes Street. Modelled on the Parthenon of Athens and designed to commemorate the fallen of the Napoleonic War, the Monument was started with insufficient funds and was never completed. The few solitary pillars are a permanent reminder of the ingratitude of the Edinburgh's citizens, the City's Folly and her lasting Disgrace.

Nevertheless, Edinburgh's history and geographical location provides a many-levelled stage for the actors in the human drama which, in the pages that follow, we shall now share ....

ART
and
ARCHITECTURE

As Scotland's Capital, Edinburgh has long been a focus for the arts. Many artists of distinction have lived and worked within its environs. This rich heritage is exhibited in the National Gallery of Scotland at the Mound, in the Scottish National Portrait Gallery, Queen Street, and the Scottish National Gallery of Modern Art at Belford Road.

The PORTRAIT PAINTER

ALLAN RAMSAY (1713-1784), the portrait painter, son of the poet of the same name, became an apprentice at the Edinburgh School of St Luke in 1729. He travelled on the Continent in 1736 and later formed the Select Society with the philosopher David Hume and the economist Adam Smith.

Ramsay was highly thought of by Dr Johnson, who said, 'you will not find a man in whose conversation there is more instruction, more information and more elegance.'

Ramsay was a friend and correspondent of Voltaire and Jean-Jacques Rousseau, and when the latter sought asylum in England in 1766, Ramsay painted his portrait for

David Hume. The writer Horace Walpole observed that whereas 'Mr [Joshua] Reynolds seldom succeeds in women, *Mr Ramsay* is formed to paint them.'

FATHER *of the* SCOTTISH LANDSCAPE

A pupil of Ramsay, **ALEXANDER NASMYTH** (1758-1840) is honoured with the title of 'Father of Scottish landscape.' He was originally an apprentice coach-builder in Edinburgh, but when Ramsay met him, he persuaded his master to cancel Nasmyth's apprenticeship. As well as painting easel-pictures, Nasmyth completed many pieces of theatrical scenery for theatres in London and Glasgow. He also had an interest in engineering. Alexander Nasmyth is buried in St Cuthbert's churchyard, Lothian Road.

JOHN KAY

The CARTOONIST

Also of considerable merit is the wickedly accurate cartoonist **JOHN KAY** (1742-1826), whose etchings of Edinburgh notables, with accompanying text, have delighted generations and are now highly collectable.

John Kay began life as a surgeon-barber, but from 1784 to 1826 he devoted himself to his

'Portraits,' which give an invaluable picture of life in the Capital during that period. Kay is buried in Greyfriars kirkyard.

SIR HENRY RAEBURN

Probably Scotland's best-known painter of this period, **Sir HENRY RAEBURN** (1756-1823), was born the son of an Edinburgh yarn-boiler. Orphaned at the age of six, he was educated at George Heriot's Hospital and apprenticed at 15 to a jeweller and goldsmith.

Sir HENRY RAEBURN

One day a seal-engraver and etcher called to see Raeburn's master and surprised the apprentice working on a portrait. The seal-engraver, David Deuchar, gave Raeburn lessons in painting and introduced him to David Martin, the leading portrait painter in Scotland at the time. Raeburn established himself in turn as the foremost portrait painter, working from his York Place studio.

On his famous visit to Scotland in 1822, George IV knighted Raeburn at Hopetoun House, near South Queensferry, and thus set the seal on his career.

Raeburn was fascinated by mechanical science, archaeology, building and gardening, and also took a keen practical interest in archery and golf. He is buried at St John's Episcopal church, off Lothian Road.

The NEW TOWN PLAN

Lord Provost GEORGE DRUMMOND (1687-1766) was the organising force behind the proposal for a New Town, and behind an 1753 Act passed for the construction of public buildings and the widening of streets. One of the main prerequisites for expansion to the north of the Old Town was the draining of the Nor' Loch, which was completed in 1759. The following year the Royal Exchange (later the City Chambers) was finished on the High Street of the Old Town. This was to provide accommodation for the city merchants who from time immemorial had carried out business in the High Street round the Mercat Cross. Covered arcades were provided for shops and coffee houses to encourage merchants to make use of the building.

Lord Provost GEORGE DRUMMOND

In 1763 Drummond laid the foundations of the North Bridge, only three years before his death. The competition for the plan for a New Town in 1776, ten years after his death, was the continuation and culmination of his life's work. Drummond is buried in the Canongate kirk.

❖

Impelled by the determined backing of the late Lord Provost Drummond's vision ('fields covered with houses, forming a splendid and magnificent city'), construction of the first New Town began in 1767, moving from the east to the west. The centre of its axis can still be seen today, the triangulation point marked into the floor of the head-quarters of the Royal Bank of Scotland at St Andrew Square. This first phase of New Town development was completed by 1800.

A competition was held to find the best plan for Edinburgh's New Town. The winner was **JAMES CRAIG** (1740-95), the son of an Edinburgh merchant, and nephew of the poet James Thomson, author of 'The Seasons.' Craig used a quotation from his uncle's famous poem to head his prize-winning 1767 plan which he dedicated to King George III.

Craig, who laid the foundation stone of the first New Town house in Rose Court, George Street on 26th October 1767, was awarded a gold medal and made a freeman of the city. King George, however, insisted that Craig's 'St Giles Street' be changed to 'Princes Street,' as the former name was an unsavoury district of London!

Another Craig plan, for improving the city of Edinburgh (1786), was rejected by the magistrates. The sole complete build-ing designed by Craig and still standing today, is the gothic Observatory House (1792) on Calton Hill, which he designed with some help from the architect Robert

Adam. Craig also laid out Merchant Street under George IV Bridge, and in 1780 worked on St Giles and the Battery at Leith.

James Craig, like George Drummond before him, did not live to see his plan for the New Town completed. In his later years he lived in obscurity and poverty, causing some resentment by appearing to trade on the reputation of his poet-uncle.

Craig's drawing instruments and copies of his plans can still be seen at Huntly House Museum, down the Royal Mile.

The ARCHITECT

ROBERT ADAM (1728-1792) was a cousin of William Robertson, principal of Edinburgh University. Born in Kirkcaldy, Adam lived a good part of his life in Edinburgh's Canongate, was educated for three years at the city's High School, and matriculated at the University at the age of 15. Some of Edinburgh's finest glories are his, including the north and south sides of Charlotte Square, Register House and part of the Old Quad of the University.

Adam's architectural aim was to 'seize … the beautiful spirit of antiquity and to transform it, with novelty and variety.'

The ENGINEER

THOMAS TELFORD (1757-1834) was born

in Dumfriesshire. He trained as a stone-mason before coming to Edinburgh in 1779. He spent two years working on the building of the New Town and Princes Street, and he used his time in the city to study its architecture with a view to improving his knowledge of civil engineering. He writes of Edinburgh: 'The grandeur of its general situation is perhaps unrivalled, and is best seen from the walks which now encompass the Calton Hill, the view comprising a great extent of fertile and well-cultivated country, a large city of romantic appearance.'

Telford carried out a number of road surveys on the Edinburgh to London route, with the intention of improving commun-ications between the cities.

However, his most striking achievement in Edinburgh is the magnificent Dean Bridge with its 90 feet span, the greatest of all his stone bridges, still standing and still in use.

Thomas Telford was known as 'The Colossus of Roads' for his achievements in building roads, docks and canals, and bridges of stone and iron. He is buried in Westminster Abbey.

The TOWN-PLANNER

Sir PATRICK GEDDES (1854-1932), a great individual, has been described as the city's 'greatest all-round citizen,' 'the Father of

British Town-planning' and an 'academic maverick.'

He was born in Ballater, near Aberdeen, and brought up in Perth where he went to school and later worked in a bank. He soon left for London where he studied for five years with the biologist T H Huxley, and also in Brittany and the Sorbonne in Paris.

Although he had previously given up studies at the Department of Botany in Edinburgh after only a week, and showed his impatience with the School of Mines in London (where Huxley taught) by betting that he could pass both elementary and advanced courses in one week (which he did after swotting through the textbooks), he was appointed Zoology demonstrator and lecturer at Edinburgh University (despite having no degree).

Sir PATRICK GEDDES

In 1886 Geddes married and took a house at 81a Princes Street. But he quickly moved into the Old Town, whose slums appalled him. Adjoining his new home at 6 James Court, Geddes bought a series of flats which he filled with students in order to encourage other residents to improve their living conditions.

Then he was passed over for promotion at Edinburgh University, but given the Chair of Botany at Dundee.

Geddes bought Ramsay Lodge at the top of the Royal Mile at Castlehill and extended it. He called it 'a seven-towered castle built for his beloved' and proceeded to build a number of Ramsay Garden flats. Next to Ramsay Lodge was Short's Observatory with its camera obscura, still accessible to the public. Geddes bought the building (known as the Outlook Tower) in 1892 and turned it into what he called a 'training ground for citizens.' The Outlook Tower was arranged as an 'index-museum' of the universe as seen from Edinburgh. Under the camera obscura was a hollow planetarium. In the Scotland Room below was a large floor-map of the country. And below it again was the Edinburgh Room, followed by surveys of Britain as a whole, Europe and the other continents. Finally, there was the World Room with two great globes, one geological and one showing vegetation.

What Geddes highlighted was the improvements which needed to be made in the environment and how to carry them out. The Outlook Tower was 'the world's first sociological laboratory.' The effects of the work of the Outlook Tower were to be seen in the first town-planning exhibitions held around 1910. Today Geddes' work is continued in the Outlook Tower by the Patrick Geddes Centre for Planning Studies.

Geddes held an interesting view—he said that the besetting sin of Edinburgh was its respectability and its culture, which was 'frozen as if in an ice-pack.'

The first CHRISTMAS CARD

Did you know that Edinburgh can lay claim to having originated the Christmas card. The laughing face of a curly-headed man was first engraved by an Edinburgh man, **ALEXANDER T AIKMAN**, for the cover of one of the ever-popular Victorian jest books. A Leith printer, **CHARLES DRUMMOND**, added the words '*A Guid New Year an' Mony o' Them*' and published it for Christmas 1841, with two outspread hands indicating a table loaded with fruit and wine. This was two years before the first Christmas card appeared in England.

BUSINESS

Today Edinburgh is one of the largest financial centres in Europe. As such it has great importance as a provider of venture capital to high technology industries. Edinburgh is the location of the headquarters of two joint-stock banks and of several merchant banks and insurance and investment companies. It is also the seat of government in Scotland and the centre of the Scottish legal and accounting professions, and plays host to the consular offices of most European countries and the United States of America.

Although banking in Scotland was first provided by religious communities, such as the Black Friars in the Cowgate and later by Italians such as the merchant Timothy Cagniole (banker to Queen Mary of Lorraine), it was Edinburgh men who really showed their financial genius.

'JINGLIN GEORDIE'

The man known as 'Jinglin Geordie' (from the sound of money clinking in his pockets), GEORGE HERIOT (1563-1623), was born in Edinburgh. Heriot's father was a prosperous jeweller and goldsmith who was Deacon-

Convener of Incorporated Trades, representing the city in the Scottish Parliament.

George was trained by his father in the most lucrative trade in the kingdom, and after his marriage in 1586, his father set him up in business in a shop off the north-east corner of St Giles kirk. In the course of time his son transferred his business to a site on the west side of the kirk. This second shop existed in Parliament Close until 1809, when the extension to the Advocates' Library meant it had to be demolished. Until that date, visitors could still see the forge and bellows. They could also see the hollow stone fitted with a stone cover for putting out the embers from Heriot's furnace when the shop was closed at night. The shop was tiny—about seven feet square.

As a goldsmith George Heriot wore the uniform of that skilled craft—a scarlet cloak with a cocked hat and a cane. But there was another side to his business which was just as financially rewarding. In 1597 he was appointed goldsmith to James VI's consort, Anne of Denmark. The appointment was proclaimed to the sound of trumpets at the Mercat Cross of Edinburgh.

In 1601 Heriot was appointed Jeweller to the King and received large fees for both royal patronages. He was now acting as cashier and banker to the King and Queen, but such was his patriotism and loyalty that he is said to have torn up and burned a

Royal bond for thousands of pounds before the King's eye as a gesture of his confidence.

It is estimated that during the ten years before James VI's accession to the throne of Great Britain, Heriot's bills for the Queen's jewels alone were not less that £50,000 in the money of the time. When James had his farewell procession down the High Street, Heriot supplied the rings and other jewels to the Scottish nobility. Two months before she joined her husband in London, Queen Anne ordered many costly items from Heriot—a pendant with diamonds, and a silver chafing dish. Heriot also charged her for lambskins to keep her jewels in. When the whole court moved to London, Heriot followed, increasing his fortune still farther.

DRINKING CUP *designed by* HERIOT

When he died in London his will was found to contain instructions for the founding of a children's home for the education, nursing and upbringing of poor orphans and fatherless children of burgesses and freemen in Edinburgh who had fallen on hard times. The Provost, Baillies and the Council and their successors were made governors of the children's hospital, the forerunner of George Heriot's School.

'BEAU' LAW

Along with fellow Scot, William Paterson

(who founded the Bank of England), **JOHN LAW** (1671-1729) was a pioneer of modern banking and founded an institution which paved the way for a national bank in France.

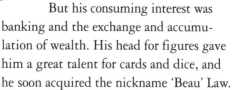

Born in Edinburgh, Law attended the High School and at his father's death, was left very well off with a goldsmith's business, the rents of a number of properties and money owed to his father by various debtors.

JOHN LAW

But his consuming interest was banking and the exchange and accumulation of wealth. His head for figures gave him a great talent for cards and dice, and he soon acquired the nickname 'Beau' Law.

When he left Edinburgh for London, he continued to gamble, but he also studied games of chance scientifically and was able to calculate the odds against a player in every game. But gambling was a night-time occupation; during the day he studied banking methods in the city.

Law became involved in a mysterious dispute over a lady, killed a man in a duel and was imprisoned and condemned to death in 1694. He was subsequently pardoned, but his opponents appealed and Law went back to prison again. Determined to escape, he cut through four bars of his cell window with a file, but he was discovered and put in irons. His trial was postponed and he managed to escape with some help in 1695, dropping thirty feet from his cell and spraining an ankle in the process.

He quickly left England for Holland, where it is thought he became secretary to the British representative there, the poet Matthew Prior. While in the country, Law visited Amsterdam to learn more about Dutch banking methods and then travelled to Paris, where he met and eloped with a married lady, whom he eventually married. Then he moved on through Switzerland to Genoa, where he settled.

In Genoa, a great Italian banking centre, Law soon made money by speculating in foreign exchange and securities; then he took himself off to Venice to make some more. Returning to Edinburgh in 1703, he settled with his wife and young son at Lauriston Castle, the family home. Whilst there he petitioned the new monarch, Queen Anne, to be allowed to return to England, but was refused.

In 1705 Law wrote an essay containing proposals for the encouragement of the Scottish economy which was debated by the Scottish Parliament. Law's plan of issuing bank notes was discussed, but his proposals were rejected, and he left Edinburgh the following year for Brussels, going on to Paris, to a France groaning under the weight of taxation and very great financial and economic problems. Once there, Law tried to persuade the French Minister of Finance to introduce bank notes into circulation.

Again, having no success, he returned to Genoa and wrote another work on political economy, and in Turin proposed the setting up of a state bank to Duke Victor Amadeus. His own finances, it must be said, had been so well managed by this time that Law was said to be worth around £100,000.

Law also developed a scheme for paying off the French national debt, which he submitted to the French Foreign Minister, but it was rejected by King Louis XIV on the grounds that John Law was not a Catholic and could not therefore be fully trusted. But Law was nothing if not persistent. All this time he had been working out his 'System' for saving the economies of nations. He announced that he had finally worked out his 'System.' When asked what it was, Law said, 'I can tell you my secret: it is to make gold out of paper.' And so, finally in 1716, his proposal for a joint-stock bank was accepted by the French Government, and as a token of his commitment to France, Law became a naturalised Frenchman.

This was the period of his greatest successes. A Company of the West was set up to represent French commercial interest in North America. This new company had exclusive trading rights with Louisiana (as well as mineral rights), and transported almost 20,000 settlers to the new territory. Louisiana at that time included much of the centre of North America: the present Louisiana, Mississippi, Arkansas, Missouri, Illinois, Iowa, Wisconsin and Minnesota— lands stretching from the Gulf of Mexico, all the way to Canada.

The Company of the West was amalgamated with the French East India Company and the China Company, and Law ordered the construction of a new town, the future New Orleans. A colossal boom in Mississippi shares now followed. Law became the first 'millionaire.'

He acquired over twenty landed properties in France (some carrying the title of Marquis). He owned large collections of jewels, a library housing 45,000 books and extensive wine cellars. He held the position of King's Secretary and was elected a member of the French Academy. Edinburgh, recognising his worth, awarded him the Freedom of the city. Law, himself, was a generous man—he gave much to charity and emptied the Paris prison of debtors.

Now a naturalised Frenchman, Law began to realise that only his religion stood in the way of an appointment to high office, so he became a Roman Catholic: in 1720, he was appointed Controller-General of Finance for the Kingdom of France. In the same year, however, his fortunes changed— an edict was issued which resulted in the devaluation of the French currency, and Law's 'System' collapsed.

He was exiled, going first to Venice and then to England, where in 1721 he persuaded Walpole to send him on a secret mission to Bavaria. He retired to Venice in 1726, spending his time attending Mass, drinking coffee, writing, reading his mail from France, gossiping, visiting antique picture dealers, attending masquerades and travelling gracefully through the canals by gondola.

The philosopher Montesquieu visited Law and observed that, 'he was still the same man, with small means but playing highly and boldly, his mind occupied with projects, his head filled with calculation.'

Law died in Venice. The scientist and socialist Saint-Simon wrote of him that 'there was neither avarice nor roguery in his composition. He was a gentle, good respectable man whom excess of credit and fortune had not spoiled ... '

BREWING

In 1749 the 16 year old **WILLIAM YOUNGER** (1733-1770) from West Linton, who had trained in the village brewery, moved to Leith. By the age of 20, he had become an exciseman. A quarter of a century later, his son **ARCHIBALD** had his own brewery in Holyrood Abbey Sanctuary. This location meant that he avoided the Town Council's two pence tax. It also gave the brewery easy access to the fine wells and springs which produced the good strong ale which he supplied to taverns such as John Dowie's in Liberton's Wynd. John Dowie's regulars like Adam Smith, or visitors like Robert Burns, found the ale 'wholesome and invigorating.' Robert Chambers wrote, 'Johnnie Dowie's was chiefly celebrated for ale —Younger's Edinburgh Ale—a potent fluid, which almost glued the lips of the drinker together, and of which few, therefore, could despatch more than a bottle.'

JOHN DOWIE'S
TAVERN
after his DEATH

By 1802 William Younger's brewery was shipping ale to the Edinburgh Ale vaults in London and had moved its premises out of the Sanctuary into the Canongate proper. Four years later the firm was brewing porter.

In 1856 **WILLIAM McEWAN** (1827-1913) started his brewery business in Fountainbridge. Seventeen years later McEwan and Younger's amalgamated.

Incidentally, it is often said that Edinburgh is eternally in gratitude to the brewing industry. The sale of beer has financed the building of such distinctive buildings as the McEwan Hall, the Usher Hall and numerous other projects.

The PRINTED WORD

As well as being a centre of the publishing and printing industry since the eighteenth century, Edinburgh has an honourable record in the production of quality newspapers. The earliest, the *Edinburgh Courant*, began in 1705 and was edited for a time by Daniel Defoe, the author of *Robinson Crusoe*. The *Edinburgh Courant* became the *Daily Courant* in 1860 but ceased publication in 1886. The *Caledonian Mercury* was founded in 1806 as an evening paper until 1867, when it was bought by the *Scotsman*.

The *Scotsman* was started in 1817 by lawyer **WILLIAM RITCHIE** (1781-1831) and a clerk in the Edinburgh Custom House, **CHARLES MACLAREN** (1982-1866). Its circulation rocketed from 1700 in 1830 to 100,000 in 1861. The *Scotsman's* evening paper, the *Edinburgh Evening News*, began production in 1873 under the direction of three men from Morayshire. The *Scotsman* is the only quality daily newspaper produced in Edinburgh, rivalling Glasgow's *Herald*.

BOOKSELLING

WILLIAM CREECH (1745-1815) was by profession a bookseller. His shop and business at the east end of the Luckenbooths had once belonged to Allan Ramsay.

Creech was also well known as a Lord

Provost of Edinburgh from 1811-1812. He served on the jury in the trial of Deacon Brodie and was the first secretary of the Edinburgh Chamber of Commerce, a position he held for many years without remuneration. He was also a co-founder of the influential literary debating club, the Speculative Society.

WILLIAM
CREECH

He was a born conversationalist and storyteller. His morning 'levées' at his home in Craig's Close, and in his shop during the afternoon, were legendary. Lord Cockburn tells us that Creech's shop was 'the natural resort of lawyers, authors and all sorts of literary idlers who were always buzzing about the convenient hive.'

Creech was also a publisher, responsible for putting the works of Adam Smith and David Hume into print. After Lord Kilmaurs introduced Creech to Robert Burns, Burns' second (Edinburgh) edition of his poems was published by Creech in 1787. At first Burns was very taken with him—'of all the Edinburgh literati and wits, he writes most like a gentleman'—but Creech angered the poet by holding back payment from the sale of his poems, until at length Burns, breathing vengeance, attacked him in print as a *little, upright, pert, tart, tripping wight ....*'

William Creech is buried in Greyfriars kirkyard.

JAMES DONALDSON (1751-1830) was born at the West Bow and in 1774 succeeded his father as proprietor and editor of the *Edinburgh Advertiser*, which enjoyed an especially wide circulation during the excitement of the French Revolution. His printing office in the Old Town was in the Stripping Close at Castle Hill—so called because criminals were stripped there before being flogged at the different public wells.

Donaldson left the bulk of his fortune—over £200,000—to found a school for 300 poor children, now known as Donaldson's School for the Deaf. A splendidly ornate building in the Tudor style, it was designed by William Playfair. In 1850 it was visited by Queen Victoria and Prince Albert.

Legend has it that Victoria wanted to buy it as a royal residence: to her dismay, the request was refused.

❖

JOHN MENZIES (1808-79) was born in Edinburgh and educated at the Royal High School. In the early nineteenth century, Edinburgh possessed some 90 booksellers as a result of the city's intellectual and cultural prominence during the Age of the Enlightenment and the Romantic Revival led north of the border by Sir Walter Scott and other writers.

As an apprentice with Sutherland the bookseller in the Calton district of Edinburgh, Menzies had to supply his own share of the coal required for heating the shop. He would be into work early to wash the stairs, sweep the pavement and clean the windows, before prayers at 8 am.

After he had finished his apprenticeship, his father gave him ten pounds and put him on a ship for London where he found work with Charles Tilt, a Fleet Street bookseller.

In 1833, after his father died, Menzies returned to Edinburgh and set up his own business at the corner of Princes Street and Hanover Street (the firm's headquarters became known as Hanover Buildings). Soon he acquired the rights to sell the works of Dickens in the East of Scotland (it is said that he was a close friend of the author, who often visited Edinburgh). He also became sole agent for the new satirical magazine *Punch*, and began to sell the *Scotsman* (normally newspapers were bought direct from the publishers by subscription).

The mid-nineteenth century saw John Menzies follow the lead of W H Smith by moving into railway bookstalls. He is buried at Edinburgh's Warriston cemetery.

PRINTING

Printing began in Scotland as a commercial process with the granting of a patent to

ANDREW MYLLAR and WALTER CHAPMAN by James IV in 1507. Following the Reformation, the General Assembly of the Church of Scotland lent its authority to the new process when it gave £200 for the purchase of printing equipment in 1562 to bring out a metrical version of the Psalms.

Native enterprise was later shown by THOMAS RUDDIMAN (1674-1757), a Banff-shire schoolmaster, who obtained employment in the Advocate's Library. In 1706, he joined up with the printer and bookseller ROBERT FAIRBAIRN to publish editions of the poems of Gavin Douglas and William Drummond, Allan Ramsay and George Buchanan. In 1730 Ruddiman became Keeper of the Advocates' Library.

PUBLISHING

ARCHIBALD CONSTABLE (1774-1827) transformed the world of publishing through his generosity to authors. He began as a young assistant in a city bookshop and by 1802 started the *Edinburgh Review* with Sydney Smith, Francis Jeffrey, Henry Brougham and Francis Horner. He also helped to publish Walter Scott's poems, and entered into a London partnership with Hurst & Robinson which sadly rendered him bankrupt a year before his death in 1827.

Archibald Constable is buried in the Old Calton burial ground, off Regent Road.

WILLIAM BLACKWOOD (1776-1834) was born in Edinburgh. He was a renowned Tory and founded *Blackwood's Magazine* in opposition to the Whig mouthpiece, the *Edinburgh Review*. It was to become a leading British periodical and remained in family editorship until its demise in 1976.

Blackwood had a keen eye for new authors. John Galt's *The Ayrshire Legatees*, for instance, first appeared in *Blackwood's Magazine*, and as a publisher Blackwood re-issued many works in book form that had first appeared in the magazine. In 1818 he published Susan Ferrier's *Marriage*. Later he published the *New Statistical Account of Scotland* (1840s), an extensive undertaking embarked upon, it was said, as much out of a patriotic impulse, as from desire for profit.

Although opposed to parliamentary reform, William Blackwood was enthusiastic about civic improvements in Edinburgh.

He is buried in the Old Calton burial ground.

❖

ROBERT CHAMBERS (1802-71), later twice Lord Provost, and his brother **WILLIAM** (1800-83), set up in business together and published *Chambers's Encyclopaedia* and *Chambers's Journal*. Robert was the author of a wide variety of non-fiction, such as *A*

Biographical Dictionary of Eminent Scotsmen, Domestic Annals of Scotland and the valuable source-book *Traditions of Edinburgh.*

William, on the other hand, initiated many city improvement schemes, involving extensive slum clearance, resulting in a significant reduction in Edinburgh's annual death rate. He also put large sums of money into the restoration of St Giles Cathedral. His statue stands in Chambers Street, the site of what had once been an insanitary huddle of old dwellings.

❖

WILLIAM SMELLIE (1745-95) was responsible for bringing out the first edition of the *Encyclopaedia Brittanica* in 1871.

Smellie was educated at Duddingston parish church and Edinburgh's High School and had developed a voracious appetite for all kinds of knowledge which gave him a truly encyclopaedic mind.

Smellie and Burns knew each other—they both sang bawdy songs at the Crochallan Fencibles, a drinking club in a local inn run by Dawnay Douglas. Burns describes him as having, *'A head for thought profound and clear, unmatch'd; Yet tho' his caustic wit was biting-rude, His heart was warm, benevolent and good.'*

William Smellie is buried in Greyfriars kirkyard.

CRIME
and
PUNISHMENT

The 'MAIDEN'

Edinburgh has the dubious distinction of having used a forerunner to the French guillotine to punish criminals. The '**MAIDEN**,' as it was known, was commissioned by the Provost, Baillies and the Town Council in 1564, and after a long lifetime of continuous use, it carried out its last execution in 1710. It is now kept in the Royal Museum, Queen Street.

As further evidence of former and very different times, we may mention the luckless student, Thomas Aitkenhead, son of an Edinburgh apothecary, who jested about the doctrine of the Trinity and was hanged in 1697 for blasphemy.

The notorious
'MAIDEN'

The SOCIETY *of* HIGH CONSTABLES

The founding date of the **SOCIETY of HIGH CONSTABLES of EDINBURGH** is generally accepted as 1611, when the magistrates were advised to elect constables, half from the merchants of the town and half from the craftsmen. Previously the functions which were now delegated to the constables had been performed by the baillies supervising four quartermasters who administered a body of 'visitors.'

The 12 officers and 26 constables appointed had a great variety of duties. They were expected to apprehend and imprison suspects, such as vagabonds and night-walkers. They were to challenge anyone in possession of a pistol or dagger and present them to the Provost and baillies for punish-ment. The constables were to intervene at times of public disorder, such as riots or street-fighting, and were given the power to break down doors to investigate noise and nuisance. They were duty-bound to search for Jesuits, seminarians, priests or 'trafficking papists,' and deal with sturdy beggars or gypsies as well as idle persons. They were empowered to deal with murders, theft or other capital crimes, and also to clear the streets and passages of filth, mid-dens and swine. They were to see that those liable for the King's service had adequate armour, and had to apprehend swearers and blasphemers in the streets, at the markets or the wells. But with such superhuman tasks before them, it is little wonder that the constables were unsuccessful in cleansing the streets where refuse lay 'like mountains' and roads had to be cut through it to the closes and booths.

The constables seemed to be used for

everything—they oversaw the sending of beggars and vagrants to the workhouse and correction house in the Calton district. They were used as tax-gatherers, as officers of the local census, for billeting soldiers and for street-patrol at Hogmany (New Year's Eve) to prevent the 'throwing of dead cats' and other riotous behaviour. They were also ordered to quell snowball fights, Chartist demonstrations and to assist at fires in the High Street or in public buildings elsewhere in the city.

The TOLBOOTH JAILS

Edinburgh's most notorious jailhouse was the TOLBOOTH beside St Giles kirk. But, situated half-way down the High Street, there was also the CANONGATE TOLBOOTH which now houses a museum—The People's Story—which is well worth a visit.

Hugo Arnot, in his *History of Edinburgh*, paints a horrific picture of the squalor of the Edinburgh Tolbooth in 1778 as 'not accommodated with ventilators, with water-pipe, with privy. The filth collected in the jail is thrown into a hole within the house, at the foot of the stair, which, it is pretend-ed, communicates with a drain; but, if so, it is so completely choked, as to serve no other purpose but that of filling the jail with a disagreeable stench .... '

The CALTON JAIL

By the late eighteenth and early nineteenth centuries, the Edinburgh Tolbooth was replaced by the CALTON JAIL, built where St Andrew's House now stands.

In 1859 William Brown, a merchant of the city, was sent to the Debtors' Prison for refusing to pay the widely unpopular annuity tax (for the upkeep of the clergy of the Established Church, normally 6 per cent of the rents of homes or shops). Brown writes that his allotted cell, No 92, was 'a small square room, 12 feet by 9 feet, the walls and roof of which were white as snow. The floor was stone. An iron bed, one chair, and a small table, comprised the furniture.'

At least there were some comforts, like the kitchen, where other petty offenders were 'all happy, some debating, some cooking and some playing draughts.' There was wholesome food available as signalled by the 'buzzing, hissing noise, arising from herring roasting, ham and steak frying. A regiment of teapots lined the upper rib of the grate, and there were a number of small tables, on which the debtors had arranged their breakfast ware.'

The THIEF

Edinburgh's most sinister and notorious criminal lived back in the eighteenth century. The father of **DEACON WILLIAM BRODIE** was a wright and cabinetmaker in the Lawnmarket and a member of the Town Council. William, his only son, succeeded to the family business in 1780. A year later he was made an ordinary Deacon of the councillors of the city.

By this time Brodie had acquired a taste for gambling, with a reputation for gambler's tricks, such as loaded dice. He spent most evenings in a gambling club in Fleshmarket Close, but was able to keep this side of his life more or less unknown and main-tain the facade of a respectable citizen.

He probably started his career of crime around 1786. In 1787 a series of robberies took place in and around the city, in which shops were broken into and goods disappeared as if by magic. There is a story that on one occasion an old lady had been too ill or tired to go to church. As she sat in her chair at home alone, a man with a black cloth over his face came into the room. He picked up the keys lying on the table, opened her bureau, took out a large sum of money from it, re-locked it, replaced the keys on the table, and, with a low bow, left the room.

Growing confident with success, Brodie and his cronies decided to break into the Excise Office. Brodie visited the office deli-

Deacon
WILLIAM
BRODIE
(*after* KAY)

berately on a number of occasions to spy out the land, learn the layout of the premises, and make an impression of the key to the outer door. On 5th March 1787 he and his accomplices made their break-in. The whole affair was a fiasco—they found only £16. At 10 o' clock the same night, the theft was discovered.

In due course one of Brodie's accomplices, who was under sentence of deportation in England, seeing the reward and pardon offered for information on the robbery, turned King's Evidence. But Brodie escaped to Dunbar on the east coast, then south again to Newcastle, London, Margate, Deal and Dover, sailing from there to Ostend.

Then he made a fatal mistake. He gave three letters to a fellow passenger to deliver to Edinburgh. The passenger, recognising the addressee as Brodie's brother-in-law, opened the letters and reported Brodie to the British Consul in Ostend. Brodie was traced to Amsterdam and arrested in an alehouse on the evening of his departure for America.

Brodie was found guilty and executed at the west end of the Luckenbooth near St Giles. He behaved with nonchalance on the gallows, his hair dressed and powdered. Twice the rope proved too short, and twice he calmly waited as it was lengthened. The third attempt was fatal.

His double life is said to have inspired R L Stevenson's *Dr Jekyll and Mr Hyde*.

Deacon Brodie is buried in the former Buccleuch church in Chapel Street.

The ANATOMIST

ROBERT KNOX (1791-1862) was the son of a mathematics teacher at George Heriot's School. His early education took place at home and then at Edinburgh's Royal High School. After graduating from Edinburgh University in 1815, he spent time in Brussels as an assistant army surgeon, tending the wounded of the Battle of Waterloo. Two years later he was at the Cape of Good Hope with the 72nd Highland Regiment during the Fifth Kaffir War. There he undertook ethnological and zoological research, collecting Bantu skulls.

Returning to Edinburgh, he became a Fellow of the Royal Society of Edinburgh, and in 1825 a Fellow of the Royal College of Surgeons and the conservator of their Museum of Comparative Anatomy and Pathology. He brought Sir Charles Bell's anatomical collection from London and soon became the foremost anatomy lecturer in Edinburgh, his classes attracting over 500 students.

However, an unfortunate association was to cloud his reputation. Knox believed that his students should be able to use fresh bodies for their studies. But there was only a limited supply legally available for dissection, which went to the University's Professor of Anatomy. They were preserved in spirits and used over and over again.

In 1827 an old man called Donal died, owing £4 rent to his landlord, the Irishman **WILLIAM HARE**. Hare persuaded a lodger, **WILLIAM BURKE**, to take the old man's body to Surgeons' Square. One of Knox's students sent Burke and Hare to Knox. They were paid £7.10s and encouraged to bring more bodies if possible.

So they proceeded to pick *live* victims this time, plied them with drink and smothered them, doing so at least 16 times. A year later, shouts of '*murder!*' prompted a police investigation which led to the horrific discovery of a woman's body still lying unpacked in a box in Knox's anatomy room.

WILLIAM BURKE
(*above*) *and*
WILLIAM HARE
(*below*)

Burke and Hare were tried for murder, and Burke was hanged in front of a large crowd. Hare turned King's Evidence and saved himself. The furious mob attacked Knox's house and burned his effigy, and he was condemned on all sides for his cynical no-questions-asked attitude. In the course of time, his fortune and reputation declined.

The POLICEMAN

JAMES MCLEVY (1801-*c*1870) was born in

Ballymacnab, County Armagh in Ireland, where he trained as a linen-weaver before coming to Edinburgh to work as a builder's labourer. He was a nightwatchman with the Edinburgh police force in 1830. Falling ill, he was taken to the Royal Infirmary where he made his first recorded arrest, that of a nurse who was secretly swigging from a bottle of wine at McLevy's bedside.

After his recovery he decided to join the police force proper and wrote number of books about his life as a policeman which gave a very vivid picture of what criminal life in Edinburgh was like. For example, during Deacon Brodie's time there had been 52 brothels between Castlehill and the top of Canongate; in McLevy's day there were notorious spots such as the 'Holy Land' and the 'Happy Land,' which McLevy describes as 'numerous dens, inhabited by thieves, robbers, thimbles, pick-pockets, abandoned women, drunken destitutes and here and there chance-begotten brats, squalling with hunger, or lying dead for days after they should have been buried.'

McLevy tells of the madame, Jean Brash: 'the house she occupied in James Square was a "bank of exchange," regularly fitted up for business. In the corner of a door-panel of every bedroom, there was a small hole neatly closed up with a wooden button, so as to escape all observation. Then the lower panels were made to slide, so that while through the peep she could see when the light was extinguished, she could by the opened panel creep noiselessly on all fours and take the watch off the side-table or rifle the pockets of the luckless person's dress.'

Sir Arthur Conan Doyle, in his characterisation of Sherlock Holmes, owes something to McLevy, for while Conan Doyle was studying medicine at Edinburgh there appeared a popular but spurious collection of crime stories by one 'James McGovan' (in reality W C Honeyman), all based on McLevy's writings. The analytical methods employed by McLevy (as recorded by Honeyman) are recognisable in the procedures of Holmes.

The MASTER *of* DISGUISE

The late **Chief Constable WILLIE MERRI-LEES** (1899-1984) was born in Leith. He was under height, short on education and had four fingers missing. But in spite of all this, he was admitted into the police force as a local lad, a rare occurrence since in those days the police force was largely made up of tall farmers or Highlanders.

He was appointed a constable in 1924 and soon acquired a reputation for 'shadowing,' which he was well able to do, for he was a master of disguise. Probably his most famous disguise was as a baby in a pram with a linen cap on his head—this was the only way he could approach a 'flasher' close enough to catch him in the act.

He moved to the Vice Squad and was required to clean up the illicit stills (shee-beens) and the considerable number of brothels in the city. On the former assign-ment he once kept the merrymakers singing near the still until the police arrived in force.

Perhaps Merrilees' greatest adventure was during the Great Kosmo Club battle in 1933. Originally known as the Bohemian Club, behind St Mary's cathedral and the Theatre Royal in the early 1920s, by 1928 it was named the Kosmo and run as a dance-hall with a curtained-off area at one end. The Kosmo girls advertised themselves in the newspapers and were sup-plied with clothing and jewellery for which they had to sign, a debt which bound them to the proprietor. Some of the girls even went to local offices and nursing homes to perform their 'services.' Willie Merrilees went so far as to disguise himself as an elderly streetwalker to be able to loiter by the club door. When the police raid took place, over 100 people were found in the club, a number acutely embar-rassed at being caught there, on account of their high standing in the community.

In 1938 Merrilees dressed as a railway

WILLIE MERRILEES, *the* MASTER *of* DISGUISE *under* COVER

porter to catch Werner Wälti, apparently a
German spy of amateurish variety. Wälti
had in his possession a German wireless
transmitter, a Mauser automatic, a national
registration card and a wireless code.
Wälti was later tried and executed as a spy.

Towards the end of his extraordinary
career Chief Constable Merrilees received
the Order of the British Empire.

The LAW

The Law in Scotland has its roots in
Roman, feudal and Germanic law. In medieval times most of Scotland's legal affairs
were conducted by churchmen. Many of
these legal figures had been educated at
Continental universities, first in France
(Orleans, Poitiers, Bourges or Paris) and (in
the seventeenth and eighteenth centuries,
until the traditional Continental connections
faded) in Holland, especially at Leiden.

Here are some Edinburgh characters of
central importance to the practice of Scots
Law.

'HARRY *the* NINTH'

HENRY DUNDAS, 1ST Viscount MELVILLE
(1742-1811), was born and educated in
Edinburgh. When he was 24, after a mere
three years as a lawyer, he was appointed
Solicitor General for Scotland. Within eight

years he became a Member of Parliament for Midlothian but lived mainly in London.

At the time of the new Government formed by the younger Pitt in 1783, Dundas was rewarded with a number of important positions—Treasurer of the Navy, President of the India Board, and after 1891, Home Secretary. Lord Henry Cockburn said that he was 'an Edinburgh man, and well calculated by talent and manner to make despotism popular ... the absolute dictator of Scotland.' Dundas was also known as 'Harry the Ninth, uncrowned King of Scotland!'

The secret of Dundas' power was the control he gained over voting and the selection of candidates—he prepared the list of representative peers. When Dundas was at the height of his power there were only 2624 county voters and 1289 burgh voters in Scotland. Edinburgh was one of three large constituencies, with 33 voters for one member.

In 1790 Dundas was returned for Edinburgh without opposition, but with the rise of radicalism in the 1790s he became unpopular. In 1806 his position was further threatened when he was impeached in Westminster Hall for embezzling public funds while Treasurer of the Navy. He was later acquitted.

Dundas is commemorated in the city by the Melville Monument designed by

William Burn, a lofty column in the middle
of St Andrew Square.

FRANCIS JEFFREY

A native of Edinburgh, **FRANCIS JEFFREY**
(1773-1850) went to the High School at
the age of eight and to the Glasgow College
at 14. Already he had developed methodical
literary habits by taking full notes of the
lectures he heard and expanding and com-
menting on them. At Glasgow he joined
the Elocution Club and exercised his skill
as a public speaker.

After graduating from Glasgow in 1789,
Jeffrey attended two classes at Edinburgh
University and then went to Oxford. But
Jeffrey found Oxford to be full of 'pedants,
coxcombs and strangers.' After a year there
he returned to Edinburgh with an English
accent. Lord Holland said that although
Jeffrey 'had lost the broad Scotch at Oxford,
he had only gained the narrow English.'

While pursuing further studies in Scots
Law at Edinburgh University, Jeffrey
declared himself disgusted with the city:
'For I am almost alone in the midst of its
swarms, and am disturbed by its filth and
debauchery, and restraint, without having
access to much of the virtue or genius it
might contain.'

Jeffrey was admitted to the Bar in 1794
and took his place in the Outer House,

which Cockburn identified as one of the chief seed-beds of Scottish culture: 'For almost two centuries this place has been the resort and the nursery of a greater variety of talent than any other place in the northern portion of our island.'

On 10th October 1802 Jeffrey and his friends gathered at his flat in Buccleuch Place, and out of their common passion for literature, politics and learning, the Whig *Edinburgh Review* was born. In the political climate of nineteenth century Britain 'the effect was electrical!' Jeffrey was chosen to be its editor.

FRANCIS
JEFFREY

When the jury system was introduced into Scotland in 1816, Jeffrey made it his business to attend almost every court in order to ensure that the new arrangements were given every chance of success by proper implementation.

By 1830 he became Lord Advocate and had some responsibility for the Reform Act of 1832. Conscious of the contrast between his ceremonial dress and his actual function as Lord Advocate, he wrote: 'You will find me glorious in a ... silk gown, and longcravat,—sending men to the gallows, and persecuting smugglers for penalties,—and every day in a wig, and most days with buckles on my shoes.' Francis Jeffrey is buried in the Dean cemetery.

'COCKY'

HENRY COCKBURN—'Cocky'—(1779-1854) attended Edinburgh's High School (which he disliked) for six years and in 1793 began his studies at the University of Edinburgh for the legal profession. In 1810 he helped to found the Commercial Bank.

Along with Francis Jeffrey and another companion, he toured the Continent in 1823, being especially struck by the beauty and decay of Venice. In the same year, with Francis Jeffrey, he helped found the Edinburgh Academy, one of the city's best known private schools.

Five years later he successfully defended Helen MacDougal, the 'wife' of William Burke in the notorious case of the body-snatchers Burke and Hare.

By 1830 Cockburn was a Solicitor General. He retired four years later, continuing to write for the *Edinburgh Review* with his long-time friend Francis Jeffrey.

Lord Henry Cockburn was appointed a Lord of Justiciary in 1837, but his greatest political contribution was, as one of the leaders of the Scottish Whigs, the drafting of the First Reform Bill for Scotland.

FRANCIS
JEFFREY

The *Edinburgh Review* of 1857 described him as 'rather below the middle height, firm, wiry and muscular, inured to active exercise of all kinds, a good swimmer, an accomplished skater, and an intense lover of the fresh breezes of heaven ... the model of a high-bred Scotch gentleman.'

Cockburn has always been considered central to Edinburgh traditions not only through his vivid description in works such as *Memorials of His Time*, but through being instrumental in preserving and celebrating what is best in the city. His name was aptly chosen for the Cockburn Association, which was founded in 1875 to foster appreciation of, and to preserve, the best of Edinburgh's buildings and environment.

Indeed Edinburgh is indebted to Lord Henry Cockburn for his protest against proposals to build on the south side of Princes Street, thus preserving the breathless view over Princes Street Gardens to the castle and the Old Town skyline. Cockburn Street is also named after him.

Lord Henry Cockburn is buried in the Dean cemetery, off Ravelston Terrace.

LORD 'COCKY' COCKBURN

LITERATURE

Perhaps it was the heady breezes of the windy city, but Edinburgh has for a long time been a place of inspiration for writers, especially poets. The list of eminent writers born in Edinburgh is so long that it is the subject of a single book alone. Here is just a sample of some of that vast talent.

The 'MAKER'

WILLIAM DUNBAR (1465-1530) is generally accepted as Edinburgh's first poet of note. A Franciscan friar, he was sent on a diplomatic mission to England by James IV to negotiate the terms of the King's marriage to Margaret Tudor. Although the ship was wrecked off the Dutch coast, Dunbar survived to accompany the ambassadors to the court of Henry VII.

A classical scholar, Dunbar combined broad satire with an early Renaissance passion for political and social allegory, often tinged with deep pessimism. Have a look at his 'Lament for the Makeris,' in which he regrets the deaths of the poets of his day—*Timor mortis conturbat me.*

The SCOTS VIRGIL

Formerly provost of St Giles kirk, **GAVIN
DOUGLAS** (1474-1522) became Bishop of
Dunkeld, but continued to live in Edinburgh. He was made a freeman of the city
in 1513 but, while on a mission to Cardinal
Wosley in London, he was accused of treason
and exiled from Scotland. His greatest poem
is a vivid translation of Virgil's *Aeneid* into
the rich Scots tongue.

The LORD LYON

Sir DAVID LINDSAY (1486-1555), Lord
Lyon King of Arms, is famous for one outstanding achievement, a satirical verse
drama entitled *Ane Satyre of the Thrie Estaits*
which attacked the oppressive feudal system
and the corruption in the society of his
time. The play was performed for Mary of
Guise in the Greenside fields below Calton
Hill. In more recent times, the play was a
great success at the Edinburgh Festival.

The GENTLE SHEPHERD

Moving centuries ahead, it was with the
genial **ALLAN RAMSAY** (1686-1758) that
Edinburgh began to enter a new golden age
of wit and literature. A native of Lanark-
shire, Ramsay (father of the portrait painter
of the same name) started his working life

as an apprentice wigmaker in Edinburgh. In 1712 he opened a wig shop in the Grass-market, but his interests and business acumen soon led him in other directions.

In 1712 he founded the Easy Club and six years later published his first collection of poems. His *Tea Table Miscellany*, a collection of Scots songs and ballads, followed in 1724, and two years later he set up a bookshop beside St Giles, at the end of the Lucken-booths. He also started the first lending library in Britain (in 1724) and finished a verse play, *The Gentle Shepherd*.

ALLAN
RAMSAY

In 1736 he founded the first regular theatre in Edinburgh and managed it until it was closed by the Licensing Act of 1737.

Later in his life he moved to an octagonal villa on the north side of Castle Hill (now Ramsay Gardens).

Ramsay was the complete professional writer, with his finger not only in prod-uction and distribution, but also in public relations and finance. He also helped revive an awareness of Scottish national culture which had been impaired by the political and religious distractions of the seven-teenth century, and, in certain circles, by admiration for English culture.

Allan Ramsay is buried in Greyfriars kirkyard.

The MAN *of* FEELING

Some Scottish writers in the eighteenth
century were actually very famous abroad.
HENRY MACKENZIE (1745-1831), novelist
and essayist, was one. He was educated at
the High School in Edinburgh and was a
lawyer by profession. He came to fame with
his novel *The Man of Feeling* (1771), an.
exercise in sentimentality which, although
it has dated badly, was the height of popularity in its day. Robert Burns wore out
two copies of it and said he prized it next
to the Bible.

Mackenzie also edited two journals, *The
Mirror* (1779-80) and *The Lounger* (1785-
87), modelled on *The Spectator*, and wrote
most of the contributions himself, showing
in his humourous observation a sharper
appreciation of human nature than in *The
Man of Feeling*, and influencing Sir Walter
Scott and John Galt. He was also the first
significant critic to praise Burns—in *The
Lounger*. His reputation was international,
but he preferred to stay in Edinburgh and
is buried in Greyfriars kirkyard.

The TRAGIC POET

ROBERT FERGUSSON (1750-74) was born in
Cap and Feather Close (now disappeared
under the North Bridge). He left St
Andrews University without a degree and

took up employment as a clerk in the Commissionary Office in Edinburgh. In 1772 he was made a member of the Old Town Cape Club and wrote two of his best poems, 'Caller Oysters' and 'Auld Reekie,' evocative portrayals of the city street life. Fergusson's promising poetic career lasted for three years until he injured himself in 1774 falling down some steps. Suffering increasingly from melancholy and madness, he was incarcerated in the Edinburgh Bedlam and died there in tragic circumstances. He is buried in the Canongate kirkyard.

ROBERT
FERGUSSON

Fergusson was much admired as a writer by both Burns and Stevenson and influenced Burns by his colourful use of the Scots tongue and the virility of his language.

'The GREAT UNKNOWN'

Sir WALTER SCOTT (1771-1832) was born at the top of College Wynd, the son of a solicitor. At 18 months he contracted polio, which left him with a permanent limp in his right leg.

He was educated at the Royal High School and Edinburgh University, and practised as an advocate in Edinburgh from 1792 to 1806. Until 1830 he held office as a Clerk to the Court of Session. Scott was

Sheriff of Selkirkshire from 1799 until his death and was created a baronet in 1820.

His first important literary work was *The Minstrelsy of the Scottish Border* (1802-3) in which he collated, adapted and arranged traditional ballads. He contributed to the *Edinburgh Review* and helped launch its rival, the Tory *Quarterly* (1809). He also wrote a series of narrative poems including *The Lay of the Last Minstrel* (in 1805), *Marmion* (in 1808) and *The Lady of the Lake* (in 1810), which were all great commercial successes.

Sir WALTER SCOTT

However, feeling a bit outshone by Lord Byron, he turned to writing historical novels, at first anonymously (as 'The Great Unknown'), the best being those set in seventeenth century Scotland. In these he nostalgically portrayed the 'heroic' values of an older civilisation and their increasing irrelevance in the coming world of commerce and order.

A desire to live 'romantically' as a landed magnate led Scott to buy Abbotsford in his ancestral Borders in 1811. This was a heavy drain on his resources, and when his publisher, Archibald Constable, experienced financial crisis, he found himself in serious debt. However, Scott paid off his debts by writing incessantly—in itself a 'heroic' act —until his death.

Quite apart from his novels (which, for example, made such a cultural impact in Europe that they inspired over 40 operas!), he had a long career as a lawyer from 1792 until his death, and also played a key role in restoring a sense of self-respect to Scotland, primarily in his stage-managing of George IV's state visit to Scotland.

The AUTHOR *of* DESTINY

SUSAN FERRIER (1782-1854) was born in Lady Stair's Close. Her father was a Writer to the Signet (solicitor), and through the circle of his friends and clients (Robert Burns among them) she met many prominent and influential men and women in the family house at Morningside. One of her father's clients was the 5th Duke of Argyll, and Susan made a number of fruitful visits to Inveraray Castle where she was able to gather some raw material for her novels.

At the castle there were amateur theatricals, large house parties and other entertainments which she recorded in her journal for later use. Another friend of her father's was Sir Walter Scott, whom her father helped at the time of the novelist's financial troubles.

She describes her time at Inveraray Castle, 'writing to my sisters three, sewing my seam, improving my mind, making tea, playing whist and numberless other duties.'

The result of this subservient role as a passive observer (common to most women of the age) was the writing of three novels: *Marriage* (1818), *The Inheritance* (1824) and *Destiny* (1831), which provide an affectionate but ironic insight into the character and manners of her society and situation.

Susan Ferrier is buried in St Cuthbert's kirkyard.

The GAEL

That the Gaelic oral tradition has survived in Scotland is largely the result of the work of **JOHN FRANCIS CAMPBELL** (1821-85). Born in Edinburgh, he spent much of his childhood in Islay which his family owned. He was a cousin of the Duke of Argyll, and his formative years were spent under the charge of John Campbell, a piper, and later in the care of the future schoolmaster Hector MacLean. Campbell also received some years of education at Eton before going to Edinburgh University to study geology and photography, and then law.

He was appointed private secretary to the Duke of Argyll who at that time held the office of Lord Privy Seal. Later he became secretary to a number of Royal Commissions, a post in which he was closely involved with the leading men of his day, one of whom, Sir George Webb Dasent, fired Campbell with a desire to record the folktales of his Gaelic-speaking homeland.

Drawing from a number of collectors, Campbell gathered together some 800 tales, publishing only a small proportion in his *Popular Tales of the West Highlands* from 1860 to 1862. As the leading authority on Gaelic folktales in Scotland, Campbell's name was put forward for the new Chair of Celtic at Edinburgh University. However he refused, preferring instead the freedom of action he enjoyed on his own, unfettered by the constraints of an organisation.

Campbell wrote of his collecting activities: 'Men who cannot read a single letter or understand a word of any language but Gaelic, ragged old paupers men might pass as drivelling idiots, begin and sing long ballads which I know to be more than three hundred years old.'

His manuscripts are now preserved in the National Library of Scotland.

The WORLD'S WORST POET

WILLIAM McGONAGALL, self-styled Poet and Tragedian (1830-1902), was born in Edinburgh of an Irish father who worked as a cotton weaver and as a hardware pedlar. William began work as a weaver in Dundee before starting out on a career as an amateur tragic actor in a travelling theatrical booth, to an amused audience of workmates.

In 1872 he gave three performances a

night as Macbeth until he was hoarse-voiced. And in Dundee's Theatre Royal he even refused to die when Macduff stabbed him: 'He maintained his feet and flourished his weapon about the ears of his adversary in such a way that there was for some time an apparent probability of a real tragedy.' (In fact, McGonagall himself had a different view of the proceedings—'the applause was deafening, and continued during the entire evening, especially so in the combat scene.')

He studied Shakespeare, Burns and Tennyson and in 1877 gave up his loom to peddle his poems in streets, shops, offices, clubs, societies and the penny gaffs (theatres). He was a figure of fun and a curiosity to amuse the drinking fraternity, and was encouraged, rather cruelly, by Edinburgh University students to take himself seriously. He describes his call to the vocation of poet thus—'A flame, as Lord Byron said, seemed to kindle up my

WILLIAM McGONAGALL

entire frame, along with a strong desire to write poetry; and I felt so happy, that I was inclined to dance.'

In 1878 McGonagall made an abortive journey to Balmoral to see Queen Victoria. He was turned back at the gatehouse, but not before he had given the sentry a taste of his power as a poet.

In 1887 he sailed to New York but was unable to get any theatrical or musical engagements. Back in Dundee he performed in circuses. He died finally in Edinburgh, having attained the dubious honour of being the world's worst poet. However, so sublimely bad is his doggerel that William McGonagall has achieved a certain immortality, and he continues to be recited with genuine enjoyment.

William McGonagall is buried in Greyfriars kirkyard.

'R.L.S.'

The Edinburgh writer with the most colourful lifestyle must be ROBERT LOUIS STEVENSON (1850-94), who was born the son of the joint engineer to the Board of Northern Lighthouses. He first studied engineering at Edinburgh University, but abandoned this for law and became an Advocate in 1875.

From an early age he was plagued by a lung infection which forced him often to travel in search of a healing climate. As a result Stevenson met his future wife in 1876 in an artists' colony in the Forest of Fontainebleau, France. Fanny Osbourne was an American, ten years older than Stevenson and at that time separated from her husband.

The following year, Stevenson made a canoe trip with the son of Dr James Young Simpson through Belgium and France. His book *Inland Voyage* was based on this experience. In 1878 he wrote *Travels with a Donkey in the Cevennes*, which describes a trip through France using a very different form of locomotion. *Treasure Island* followed in 1883. Then came *Kidnapped* and *The Strange Case of Dr Jekyll and Mr Hyde* (1886), written when he was in Bournemouth.

In 1888 Stevenson chartered a yacht to sail the Pacific. He went to Tahiti and to Hawaii. There, in a hut on the beach, he finished *The Master of Ballantrae*. Later he went on to the Gilbert Islands and Samoa and to Australia. But it was Samoa that Stevenson finally settled on, where he built a fine house, farmed his estate and continued to write. His novel, *Weir of Hermiston* was unfinished at his death.

The CREATOR *of* SHERLOCK HOLMES

SIR ARTHUR CONAN DOYLE (1859-1930) belonged to an Edinburgh family of Irish descent. He studied medicine at Edinburgh and distinguished himself in rugby, cricket, boxing, ski-ing and motor-racing.

But he is known best as the writer of the world famous novels based on the investigations of the detective Sherlock

Holmes who lived in London at 221b Baker Street with his assistant Dr Watson.

Arthur Conan Doyle wrote four Sherlock Holmes novels and 56 stories, taking the characteristic method of investigation from his experience of the well-known Edinburgh surgeon, Dr Joseph Bell, and perhaps also from the case histories of the Edinburgh detective McLevy (as re-worked by James McGovan, alias W C Honeyman, in his popular novel *Brought to Bay*).

Sir ARTHUR CONAN DOYLE

Conan Doyle, who had been a field surgeon in the Boer War, was responsible for a number of technical innovations. He persuaded the Army to use tin helmets, and introduced inflatable lifejackets to the Navy. He was interested in the reform of the divorce and criminal law, and promoted women's rights and inter-racial marriage; he also advocated the construction of a Channel tunnel. In 1900 and 1906 he stood twice unsuccessfully for Parliament for Edinburgh and the Borders. He was also a special adviser to the police in a number of criminal cases. In later life Conan Doyle became fascinated by the supernatural and lectured on the subject.

MEDICINE

The HISTORY

The emergence of professional men of
medicine in Edinburgh was a gradual one.
We hear first of all of an apothecary's shop
in 1450, in one of the early High Street
Luckenbooths. Then in 1505 the Royal
College of Surgeons was founded from the
Corporation of Barber-Surgeons, receiving
its charter from James IV in 1506 (the
College is now housed in Surgeons' Hall in
Nicolson Street, built in 1833 from a
William Playfair design).

The Royal College of Physicians was
founded in 1681 (its premises are now in
Queen Street in a building designed in 1844
by Thomas Hamilton, the facade adorned
with statues of Hippocrates, Aesculapius
and Hygeia).

The GREGORYS

Edinburgh is famous for two extraordinary medical and scientific
families. The first, the **GREGORYS**
had eight outstanding members—
Dr John Gregory was Professor of
the Practice of Physic at Edinburgh
from 1766 until his death in 1773.

His grandfather had been the first Professor of Mathematics at Edinburgh, a friend of Isaac Newton and was the inventor of the reflecting telescope. His father was Professor of Medicine at King's College in Aberdeen. His son James held the Chair of Medicine at Edinburgh; his grandfather's brother David was a doctor and inventor whose son, also David, became Savilian Professor of Astronomy at Oxford in 1962. A third David was Professor of Mathematics at St Andrews, a post also held by John's great-uncle, Charles.

However, the family is probably best remembered for the highly popular patent medicine, 'Gregory's Mixture,' made from magnesia, rhubarb and ginger, which soothed generations of upset stomachs.

As a matter of interest, Professor James Gregory is buried in Canongate kirkyard.

The MONROS

The MONROS had three shining lights— Alexander Primus, Secundus and Tertius, whose tenancy of the Chair of Anatomy at Edinburgh lasted from 1719 to 1846.

Monro Primus was a brilliant anatomist who became Professor of Anatomy at 21. It was he who established the reputation of the Edinburgh School of Medicine as a centre of international importance. It is reported that such was his pre-eminence

that, in the nineteenth century, his grand-
son still dutifully read his grandfather's
lecture notes *verbatim* to his long-suffering
students, without any regard whatsoever to
the irrelevance of some of the material.

Alexander Monro Primus and Secundus
are buried at Greyfriars kirkyard, and
Monro Tertius at the Dean cemetery.

The PIONEER *of* DIET

JAMES LIND (1716-94) was born in the city
and educated at the University of Edinburgh. He joined the Navy as a surgeon's
mate, serving on the Guinea coast, in the
Mediterranean, in the West Indies and on
the Channel fleets.

During his service he kept detailed
records of the diseases he had to treat. He
was particularly concerned about the serious
outbreaks of scurvy in 1740-44 during
Anson's circumnavigation of the globe.
Three years later he conducted a controlled
trial on board 'HMS Salisbury,' and was
able to demonstrate conclusively the power
of oranges and lemons to cure and prevent
scurvy. His conclusions were published in
his *Treastise on the Scurvy* (1753), one of the
world's classic medical texts. Within two
years of the general introduction of lemon
juice in 1795, scurvy virtually disappeared
from the Navy.

Lind's hygienic measures also eliminated

typhus, and his recommendation of a high-energy protein diet with a high-fibre content had a revolutionary effect on naval and military health, and in due course on dietary practices in civilian life. Lind was also the first to identify the signs of hypothermia from exposure and immersion, and the first to warn against the fatal effect of administering alcohol in such cases. He further advocated intermittent chest compression and mouth-to-mouth resuscitation for those rescued from the water.

ANDREW DUNCAN

ANDREW DUNCAN (1744-1828) was a St Andrews man who studied medicine at Edinburgh and then travelled to China as a Company surgeon with the East India ship 'Asia.'

In 1770 he settled in Edinburgh and started his practice, also founding the Aesculapian Society for the promotion of business and good relations between physicians and surgeons.

In 1789 he became President of the Royal College of Physicians, and, in the following year was given the Chair of Physiology at Edinburgh. He campaigned for the institution of a Chair in Medical Jurisprudence, to which his son was eventually appointed.

In 1807 came the Royal Charter for the

asylum which he had been so instrumental in promoting. It is believed that his plan to establish a lunatic asylum in the city may have been inspired by the wretched death of the poet Robert Fergusson.

Andrew Duncan is remembered by the Clinic at Morningside which bears his name, and he is buried in the Buccleuch cemetery, off Chapel Street.

The 'NAPOLEON of SURGERY'

JAMES SYME (1799-1870) was born in Edinburgh and attended the University as a medical student. He was appointed to the Chair of Clinical Surgery, and earned the title of the 'Napoleon of Surgery,' the greatest surgeon of his day.

Something of the atmosphere of medicine in his time is captured in the *Edinburgh Hospital Reports* of 1893 where one of Syme's house-surgeons describes his superior at one of his well-attended lecture days in 1853:

Professor
JAMES SYME

'[Syme] comes in, sits down with a little, very little bob of a bow, rubs his trouser legs with both hands open, and signs for the first case. The four dressers on duty, and in aprons, march in (if possible in step), carrying a rude wicker basket, in which, covered by a rough red blanket, the patient peers up at a great amphitheatre crammed with faces. A brief description, possibly the case had been discussed at a former lecture, and then the little, neat, round-shouldered, dapper man takes his knife and begins, and the merest tyro sees at once a master of his craft at work—no show, little elegance, but absolute certainty, ease and determination; rarely a word to an assistant—they should know their business if the unexpected happens; his plans may change in a moment, but probably only the house-surgeon finds it out; the patient is sent off, still anaesthetised, and then comes a brief commentary, short, sharp and decisive, worth taking verbatim if you can manage it; yet he has no notes, a very little veiled voice and no eloquence .... '

James Syme is buried in St John's churchyard, Princes Street.

The GYNAECOLOGIST

Bathgate was the birthplace of **JAMES YOUNG SIMPSON** (1811-70), but he began his studies at the University of Edinburgh at the tender age of 14. Before the age of 30, he was appointed Professor of Midwifery and in 1847 he made the momentous discovery of the anaesthetic properties of chloroform, as James Miller, in his *Principles of Surgery* (1852), relates:

'Late one evening ... on returning home

after a weary day's labour, Dr Simpson, with his two friends and assistants, Drs Keith and Matthews Duncan, sat down to their somewhat hazardous work in Dr Simpson's dining-room. Having inhaled several substances, but without much effect, it occurred to Dr Simpson to try a ponderous material, which he had formerly set aside on a lumber-table, and which, on account of its great weight, he had hitherto regarded as of no likelihood whatever. That happened to be a small bottle of chloroform. It was searched for, and recovered from beneath a heap of waste paper. And, with each tumbler newly charged, the inhalers resumed their vocation.

Doctor
JAMES
YOUNG
SIMPSON

'Immediately an unwonted hilarity seized the party; they became bright-eyed, very happy and very loquacious—expatiating on the delicious aroma of the new fluid. The conversation was of unusual intelligence and quite charmed the listeners —some ladies of the family and a naval officer, brother-in-law of Dr Simpson.

'But suddenly there was a talk of sounds being heard like those of a cotton-mill, louder and louder; a moment more, then all was quiet, and then—a crash. On awaking, Dr Simpson's first perception was mental —*This is far stronger and better than ether,* said he to himself. His second was to note that he was prostrate on the floor, and that among the friends about him there was both confusion and alarm. Hearing a noise, he turned round and saw Dr Duncan beneath a chair; his jaw dropped, his eyes staring, his head bent half under him; quite unconscious, and snoring in a most determined and alarming manner.'

Simpson inspired such confidence in his discovery that chloroform was administered to Queen Victoria in 1853 at the birth of Prince Leopold. Simpson had, in effect, founded the modern practice of gynaecology and, having been made Physician to the Queen in Scotland in 1847, was created a baronet in 1866. He is buried at Warriston cemetery.

The PIONEER of ANTISEPTIC

JOSEPH LISTER (1827-1921) was born in London and was a graduate of University College, London. He went to Edinburgh in 1853 to work as an assistant to the aforementioned James Syme, occasionally performing surgery in the Edinburgh Royal Infirmary. The next year he was appointed a lecturer in surgery at the Royal College of Surgeons. His day was one of routine and hard work: 'I get up by alarm at 5.30 and light my fire ... My coffee boils while I dress. I take it and a bit of bread, work for three or four hours and set off to my 10 o' clock lecture when my mind is brim full of it.'

Lister was also in the habit of visiting an Edinburgh slaughterhouse to conduct experiments in blood coagulation.

He married Professor Syme's daughter in 1856 and then went to Glasgow as Regius Professor of Surgery. Nine years later he learned that Louis Pasteur had written a paper on fermentation and rotting, pointing out the role of dirt in breeding microbes. Some time after this, Lister heard that carbolic acid was being used in Carlisle for purifying sewage. Putting the two ideas together, he used a carbolic spray during his serious operations, and it proved successful in reducing infection and fatalities.

When Syme retired in 1869, Lister took his place as Professor of Surgery in the city. He built up an enormous private practice, working at the same time on other ideas, such as more effective dressings made from muslin gauze which he had found in an Edinburgh drapery store.

However, in due course Lister left Edinburgh for King's College Hospital, London where he took up the post of Professor of Surgery. By this time antisepsis was being used more and more widely.

He was made a baronet in 1883 and retired ten years later. In 1898 he was presented with the Freedom of Edinburgh. He was the first doctor to be made President of the Royal Society, and the first to receive a peerage.

WOMEN *in* MEDICINE

The contribution of women to the practice of medicine in Edinburgh has been of great significance—but it was not always so. At first women were barred from studying medicine, but there were some who would not take no for an answer.

SOPHIA JEX-BLAKE (1840-1912) was one such pioneer. She adopted a more frontal attack on that bastion of male privilege. In 1869 she approached the Faculty of Medicine at Edinburgh with a request to study medicine, having already completed two years of a medical course in the States. When they got wind of her application, the medical students staged a riot to keep women from their classes at the Surgeons' Hall.

However, in 1872 a judgment was given in favour of seven female applicants to the Medical Faculty which had formerly refused to award graduate degrees to women. Unfortunately this judgment was reversed by the Court of Session, and it took a Parliamentary Bill in the following year to clear the way in the medical profession for the female sex.

Meanwhile, Dr Jex-Blake did not stand

idly by. She graduated MD at Berne in Switzerland and founded the London School of Medicine for Women. She set up the first dispensary for women and children at 4 Manor Place, Edinburgh, where she worked for 21 years as a general practitioner. In 1886 she became Dean of the Women's Medical College in Surgeon's Square and helped to found the Edinburgh Hospital for Women and Children (the Bruntsfield).

Dr ELSIE INGLIS (1864-1917), the Edinburgh woman surgeon, died in 1917 at the age of 53, having sailed into Newcastle after service with the Scottish Women's Hospitals field unit on the Serbian Front. During her first tour in Serbia she was operating on the wounded for 58 hours out of 63. She helped Serbian doctors to combat typhus and typhoid fever; it was dangerous work and many doctors died.

In her second spell of duty in Serbia she was captured by the Austro-Hungarian army and then repatriated. After the war the Serbs built a monument to Dr Inglis and her staff; and the Yugoslav administration awarded her their highest honour (never before awarded to a woman), the Order of the White Eagle, to which were added 'the swords' after her death. The Russians, whose troops she had also treated, gave her the St George Medal for bravery, and the French decorated her for valour. Elsie Inglis had trained at Edinburgh University, where she was one of the first women medical students, but she had become so dissatisfied with the lack of proper tuition for women that in 1892 she set up her own medical school for women.

In 1902 Elsie Inglis opened a hospice for mothers and children from the slum areas of Edinburgh. This became the Elsie Inglis Memorial Hospital after her death in 1917.

Doctor
ELSIE INGLIS

Dr Inglis, who is buried in the Dean cemetery, also founded the Scottish Women's Suffragette Federation.

MILITARY

Edinburgh's recorded military history begins around the year AD 600 when a cavalry force of 300 men rode south from the fortified town of Eidyn, the home of the ruler of the Gododdin, King Mynyddog.

The hand-picked and disciplined troops were well armoured in coats of mail and trained in the traditions of the departed Roman army. They spent a number of months being entertained at a hospitable fort. When they reached Catterick they attacked the English and tragically were annihilated. The poet Aeirin was apparently the only survivor—the lines he wrote on the battle forms the oldest Scots poem.

The MARQUIS *of* MONTROSE

JAMES GRAHAM, Marquis of MONTROSE (1612-50) was an astute general who fought against the Covenanting armies between 1644 and 1645. Montrose was implacably opposed to Archibald Campbell, the 8th Earl and 1st Marquis of Argyll (known as 'Gillespie Gruamach'), suspecting him of wanting to rule Scotland in place of Charles I. Certainly Argyll was the most powerful member of the Committee of Estates which governed Scotland at the time, and attacked those who would not sign the Covenant.

In spite of Montrose's flair for generalship and his success in what appeared to be impossible tactical conditions (he defeated a Covenanter army three times the size of his own using only his 'naked, weaponless, amunitionless men'), he was finally defeated in Sutherland and found wounded and exhausted among its bogs and icy streams.

In Edinburgh he was sentenced to death, 'to be … hanged up on a gallows Thirty Foot high, for the space of Three Hours, and then to be taken down, his head to be cut off upon a Scaffold, and hanged on Edinburgh Tolbooth; his Legs and Arms to be hanged up in other public Towns of the Kingdom, his body to be buried at the Place where he was executed.'

The Town Guard escorted him to the place of execution (commanded by Major Thomas Weir, later tried and executed as a wizard). As he passed up the Royal Mile, Montrose came to Moray House and the cavalcade stopped—looking up, he caught sight of his enemy Argyll gloating through the shutters. Montrose was eventually laid to rest in St Giles kirk.

Having crowned the next king, Charles II, at Scone, Argyll took sides with Cromwell against him. Argyll was finally defeated and beheaded at Edinburgh in 1661.

The PORTEOUS RIOTS

'JOCK' PORTEOUS, after whom the notorious
Porteous Riots of 1736 were named, was the
son of a tailor in the Canongate. He was
trained by his father to follow his profession,
but at an early age showed signs of disrup-
tive behaviour and rebelliousness—so much
so, that he attacked his father in temper.
His father could not put up with him any
longer and sent him off to serve with the
Scots Dutch Brigade in the States of
Holland, fighting for Queen Anne. There
Jock 'found himself.'

Although shooting a hen for amusement
was his only warlike act in Flanders, he was
suspected of having cut the throat of his
captain after the latter had given him a
beating. Porteous left the army shortly after
and returned home.

At the time of the 1715 Jacobite Rising
the number of Edinburgh's Town Guard
was increased, and the trained bands and
volunteers were also given arms. The 'black
banditti,' as Robert Fergusson called them,
accepted Jock Porteous as the Guard's drill-
master on the strength of his service in the
Low Countries.

Although dismissed and then reinstated
(possibly over another outburst of temper),
in 1718 he was made ensign of the Town
Guard, which was by then composed of 100
men divided into three companies, each

commanded by a captain-lieutenant. In 1726 Porteous was appointed captain-lieutenant and paraded in front of his men in their military coats and cocked hats, carrying muskets, bayonets and Lochaber axes (a sort of halberd with a hook).

From his appointment Porteous was unnecessarily harsh, abusing his authority. He was contemptuous of the common people, and they knew to be wary of him. A broad-shouldered, muscular man, with a gentle-seeming but pockmarked face, he had an ability to intimidate which won him the full support of the Town Council.

EIGHTEENTH CENTURY CAPTAIN *of the* TOWN GUARD (*after* KAY)

Porteous' fortunes soured when a smuggler named Andrew Wilson appeared on the scene. The people of Scotland sided with smugglers and hated excisemen because they saw taxes as yet another instrument of oppression from London. Wilson had cornered a collector of excise in his lodgings after he had gone to bed. He and his friends began to break down the door, but the collector jumped out of the window with a bag of money, unfortunately leaving his trousers behind. He lay hiding under some straw until morning, dressed only in his nightshirt.

Meanwhile Wilson and his accomplices were arrested and taken to the Tolbooth and sentenced to be hanged. At that time convicted criminals were hanged in the Grassmarket at the foot of the West Bow, the gallows placed in a massive block of sandstone with a triangular socket. After Wilson was hoisted up on the gallows, the magistrates present went to a tavern overlooking the gallows for the 'deid-chack,' the customary execution meal. After half an hour the criminal was cut down, the signal being given by the magistrates pointing a white rod out of the tavern window. As he went to cut Wilson down, the hangman was stoned and one of the mob cut the rope. Immediately a shower of stones and dirt was thrown at the Guard, who opened fire in retaliation, killing three and wounding twelve, and then withdrew up the West Bow chased by the crowd. They fired again and three more were killed.

Porteous, put on trial for the episode, was found guilty but was reprieved by the Queen Regent. The Edinburgh mob were so incensed that they went on the rampage, stealing the keys of the West Port, nailing and locking the gates, and then streaming down the Cowgate to lock all the other gates in order to stop the regular troops getting into the town. They broke into the Guard House and took 90 firelocks, Lochaber axes and the town drums, freed a number of prisoners and tried to break into the Tolbooth with sledgehammers. When

this proved impossible they set fire to the
gates with barrels of tar.

Captain Porteous was dragged into the
street, a coil of rope was taken from a shop
in the West Bow, and he was strung up on
a dyer's drying-frame (about 15 feet high).
After he had hung for three minutes, the
crowd stripped off his nightgown, broke
his arm and shoulder with a Lochaber axe,
burned his foot and then jerked him up
and down for an hour. Finally they nailed
down the rope and left his body hanging
till five o' clock the next morning.

Jock Porteous was a violent man in a
violent town. He is buried in Greyfriars
kirkyard, off Candlemaker Row.

The 'PIRATE'

JOHN PAUL JONES (1747-1792), known as
'the Pirate,' was born in Kirkcudbrightshire.
He was apprenticed at the age of twelve to
a Whitehaven merchant and made a number
of voyages to America where he had an
elder brother in Virginia.

Having been a mate on a slave-carrying
ship, he inherited his brother's property in
1773 and changed his name, John Paul, to
John Paul Jones. In 1775 he volunteered
for service with the American fleet and was
posted to Europe two years later.

In September of that year Jones' ship
arrived off the coast of Eyemouth and sailed

passed Dunbar, then close to Leith on its way to Kirkcaldy. Alert to trouble, the people of Leith worked furiously through the night to prepare for an invasion. Old cannons were rolled into position, barricades were built, soldiers and seamen manned the coastal defences along the shore. By this time Jones knew that Leith was virtually defenceless and that the guns at Edinburgh Castle could not be fired in the direction of the port.

He planned to demand £200,000 from the citizens of Leith, and wrote to them—'I do not want to distress the poor inhabitants; my intention is only to demand your contribution towards the reimbursement which Britain owes to the much injured citizens of the United States ....'

But the letter was never sent, for the wind changed (some said through the prayers of a local minister), and the Americans were forced to move on.

Jones went on also to serve in the French and Russian Navies, and died in Paris.

EARL HAIG

DOUGLAS, 1st Earl HAIG (1861-1928) was born in Edinburgh, and educated at Clifton and at Brasenose College, Oxford, before going to Sandhurst in 1883. Then he travelled to India with the 7th Hussars. Despite failing examinations for Staff College and suffering from colour blindness, his career was meteoric.

He served with the Egyptian Cavalry in the Omdurman Campaign in 1898 and was a Brigade-Major in the Boer War before commanding the 1st Cavalry Brigade at Aldershot and being posted to South Africa. From 1900, after only 15 years service, he became a column commander in the Cape Colony and Regimental Lieutenant-Colonel with the 17th Lancers. In 1903 he was Inspector-General of Cavalry

Earl HAIG

in India, and in the following year became a Major-General. He went to the War Office in 1906 as Director of Military Training, and then in 1909 returned to India as Chief of the General Staff.

At the time of the First World War he took two divisions to France as the 1st Corps and enhanced his reputation as a leader during the first Battle of Ypres. He was then appointed Commander-in-Chief.

But despite the arithmetical progression of his career to this point, his reputation suffered as a result of decisions he took during the War. Although he had courage and skill in directing the battle, and played an important part in the defeat of the enemy, arguably he failed to make himself aware of the tactical situation on the ground and pointlessly committed the lives of many of his men where there was little chance of success.

Nevertheless, after the War he worked tirelessly for the development of the British Legion and the United Services Fund. His equestrian statue stands on the Edinburgh Castle Esplanade and there is a fine display in his memory at Huntly House Museum.

'MONS MEG'

And by way of a parting shot—the famous attraction at Edinburgh Castle is 'MONS MEG,' the massive late medieval siege cannon made for King James II in 1455. It was believed that she had been made locally for the siege of Threave Castle in Kirkcudbrightshire, but now Mons Meg is thought to have been made at Mons in Flanders.

In 1558 she was fired on the occasion of the marriage of Mary, Queen of Scots to the Dauphin of France—the cannon ball was found two miles away. And Mons Meg finally burst when firing a salute for James VII, the former Duke of York, in 1682.

In 1754 she was removed to London, but, through the efforts of Sir Walter Scott, was returned to Edinburgh in 1829. In 1985, returning to London, this time for restoration, she yielded new information about herself—the 13 ft 4 inch gun with the 20 inch bore weighed in at 5.94 tons.

MUSIC

Edinburgh, as the capital of Scotland, has always been rich in music, both instrumental and vocal, whether classical, folk or music-hall. However, the only professional opera singer from Edinburgh to achieve an outstanding international reputation is the subject of this next character sketch.

EDINBURGH'S CARUSO

JOSEPH HISLOP (1884-1977) began his career at the age of ten when he joined the choir of St Mary's Episcopal Cathedral. After leaving the Cathedral School, he went into the photo-process engraving trade, eventually going to London to study colour photography.

He then received an offer of a visit to Sweden in 1907, to introduce 3-colour reproduction to a printing firm in Gothenburg. There he joined a male voice choir, eventually becoming an occasional soloist. A visiting professional singer happened to hear Hislop sing and suggested that he audition for Dr Gillis Bratt, a famous singer and throat specialist. Hislop passed the audition and began a period of study with

Dr Bratt which culminated in his joining
the Opera School attached to the Royal
Opera House in Stockholm.

In 1914 Hislop made his debut
as Faust in Gounod's opera of the
same name, and then went to
London to make a number of
recordings for the HMV record
company under the Zonophone
label. While in London he saw
Caruso at Covent Garden and, after
the performance he was able to get
Caruso's autograph in an Italian restaurant.
Caruso was interested to meet the young
Scottish tenor making his reputation in
Sweden.

JOSEPH HISLOP

Hislop made his Covent Garden debut
in 1920 as Rodolfo and on the opening
night was conducted at short notice by
Sir Thomas Beecham. The following day
he was introduced to Puccini, who had
been in the audience. Hislop records, 'I
was completely bowled over by the very
complimentary things he said about my
performance, which of course delighted me.'

Hislop sang a number of major and
memorable roles during his distinguished
career. At the end of his stage career he
returned to Stockholm, where he remained
from 1936 to 1948, teaching at the Royal
Academy of Music there. Then, upon his
return to the United Kingdom, Hislop
taught at the Guildhall School of Music

and was an adviser in vocal production at both Covent Garden and Sadler's Wells.

Joseph Hislop, ending his days in the Fife region, lived to the ripe old age of 93.

SIR HARRY LAUDER

For many years a vigorous undercurrent of popular musical entertainment flourished in the 'penny gaffs' and the 'free and easys' of the town entertainers.

Sir HARRY LAUDER (1870-1950) is to-day a figure of contradiction—his baroque caricatures of the humours of Scotland either endear or cause revulsion. As to his success, there can be no disagreement. Chatting once to Caruso, Lauder was amazed at the astuteness of the Italian tenor over royalties. His own songs had been signed away, often for a pound a song. When it is

Sir HARRY LAUDER *in* STAGE DRESS

considered that the biggest record sellers in the world were Melba, Caruso and Harry Lauder, the Scotsman's reputation for meanness can be seen to be particularly ironic.

Lauder was born in a very humble birthplace by the sea at Portobello. When he was twelve years old the family moved to England, as his father had taken up an offer of employment there. In 1882, however, his father died, and the family moved back to Scotland, this time to Arbroath where Harry joined the Band of Hope and learned to sing hymns and songs and give recitations. At the age of 13 he won a singing competition.

By 1894 Lauder, through talent and determination, had become a professional entertainer in Glasgow. In 1895 he toured Scotland with the violinist Mackenzie Murdoch, and then toured for six weeks as a comedian, but also as a baggageman, billposter and stage carpenter—he learned the craft of the theatre from A-Z.

In 1900 he went to London and after some anxious weeks was suddenly summoned to replace a 'turn' who had gone sick from Tommy Tinsley's revue 'Gatti's in the Road.' Lauder hit his audience with everything he knew. Dressed in tartan trousers, yellow spats, brown boots, coloured waistcoat and black frock-coat, he sported a black and green tie and a badly-fitting tile hat. The critics were pleased: 'This man … brings the scent of the Scottish heather over the footlights into the smoke-laden atmosphere of the music-hall.'

Seven years later Lauder's popularity was such that he was able to make the first of his many trips to the United States. Lauder played the New York Theatre in Times Square for over $4500 a week. In 1908 he was at the Lincoln Square Theatre and followed his huge successes with 22 trips to North America, being welcomed into the highest levels of American society, and making friends with such notable figures as Henry Ford.

He was now earning more than any other star. One of his supporting artists was the then unknown songwriter Irving Berlin.

Lauder's philosophy was simple: 'If, by bein' a simple Scots comic, and singin' bonnie humorous songs, I can do my wee bit to help make the world a brighter place, and help mysel' along the road at the same time, well, then, I'm richt glad to lend a hand.'

MYSTERY

Throughout history there have been those who have considered Edinburgh to be two-faced. The city which gave birth to the creator of *Dr Jekyll and Mr Hyde* (based on the sweet and sour Deacon Brodie), for long presented an image of contradiction that anticipated modern psychoanalysis and had its roots deep in the human psyche.

The FLODDEN HERALDS

Legend relates that in 1513, around mid-night before the Battle of Flodden, while the cannon were being trundled out of the castle and down the Royal Mile, spectres of heralds were seen at the Mercat Cross, proclaiming the list of the 10,000 men who were destined to die in the battle, intoning their names to the terrified population.

An AFFAIR *of the* HEART

A century later, another unusual case of premonition took place in Edinburgh— this time an affair of the heart. Lady Eleanor Campbell, the young wife of the brutal Viscount Primrose, did not have an easy marriage. One morning, as she was dressing in her first floor chamber, she saw in the mirror her husband creeping towards her, a knife in his hand, as if to kill her. She immediately made for the window and jumped into the street below. Luckily she survived the fall and she hurriedly left her husband and escaped to her relatives.

Viscount Primrose then went abroad and for many months Lady Eleanor heard nothing. Then one day a fortune-teller came to Edinburgh. Lady Eleanor was persuaded to visit the fortune-teller and asked for news of her husband. She was taken to a mirror, and when she looked into it she saw her husband in a church, dressed as a bridegroom about to marry. Suddenly she saw her brother arrive and attack Lord Primrose.

Lady Eleanor wrote down exactly what she had seen, dated and sealed the account before a witness and had the paper locked away. It was only when her brother returned from travel on the Continent that she discovered that he had been in Amsterdam and there heard of a noble Scotsman who was about to marry the daughter of a family he knew. When Lady Eleanor's brother went to the church, he found to his astonishment that the bridegroom was in fact his brother-in-law. Everything went as the vision in the mirror suggested, but the ceremony was stopped before the bigamous marriage could take place.

When Lady Eleanor examined the document she had signed, describing her vision in the clairvoyant's mirror, she found it was dated the very day on which her brother had broken up Lord Primrose's second wedding. The facts of this case are worth taking seriously, as the story was recorded both by Robert Chambers the writer and publisher, and Sir Walter Scott.

MARY KING'S CLOSE

When the new Royal Exchange (the present City Chambers) was built for the merchants of Edinburgh, it was constructed over some of the old closes. One of these, Mary King's Close, can still be seen by guided parties, under the present level of the Royal Mile, a reminder of what Old Edinburgh was once like.

The plague of 1645 killed most of the residents in Mary King's Close and so it was abandoned, every door and window closed and shuttered. Soon there were rumours of phantoms and headless bodies seen through chinks in the shutters, all glowing with a ghastly blue light. In 1750 fire destroyed the upper part of the Close and three years later it was incorporated into the Royal Exchange, the lower end of the Close being demolished to make way for Cockburn St.

In the late eighteenth century, Thomas Coltheart, a law agent, and his wife, lived in the Close. One Sunday afternoon, when her husband was not feeling well and had gone to bed, Mrs Coltheart sat reading her Bible. She glanced up for a moment and to her horror saw a ghastly head floating in the room, looking at her with sightless eyes. Her husband did not believe her, but he also saw the head, and then a child and an arm, all suspended in the air. In spite of prayer, the phantoms increased in number until the room was full of them. Then suddenly there was a deep groan and everything vanished as quickly as it came.

In later times simple explanations were found for some alleged sightings, for the workrooms and shops of the Close were occupied during the nineteenth century. The Edinburgh Company's Oyster Bar flourished from 1754 to 1897 and the Chesney family repaired and sharpened saws which they hung from hooks in the roof. The Close being built over the Nor' Loch, the eerie blue light sighted was nothing more sinister than marsh gas which burned with a blue flame.

The CASTLE

After Charles II's coronation at Scone in 1651, Cromwell's army marched on the city and a special detachment was garrisoned in the Castle. In the middle of the night a lonely sentry heard the sound of a drum,

the thud of marching feet and an old Scots
march. He challenged but got no answer,
so he fired his musket. His commanding
officer did not believe his story, and the
sentry was replaced. After a time spent on
guard duty, late into the night, the second
sentry heard an old Scots march, then an
English one, then a French. He fired and
there was nothing—only a deathly silence.

The MIDNIGHT GHOST

When General Robertson Lawers (who
had served through the American Wars of
Independence) rented an old building
known as the Wrights Houses (near what
are now the Meadows) in 1792, his negro
servant 'Black Tom' complained of seeing a
midnight ghost in the shape of a headless
lady carrying a child in her arms. Around
the turn of the next century, the Merchant
Company bought the property and demolished it. When the old stone floor was
pulled up, the workmen found the headless
skeleton of a woman and the skeleton of an
infant beside her, wrapped up in a lace-
trimmed pillowcase. It seems that this was
the French wife of James Clerk who had
been given the house by his father in 1664.
When James went abroad to fight in the
army, he left his wife and young baby in the
care of a brother who, when he heard his
brother had been killed in battle, promptly

murdered his sister-in-law and niece.

The WHITE LADY

When the moon shines over Corstorphine, the figure of a woman dressed in white can sometimes be seen, wearing a white hood and carrying a sword dripping with blood. The White Lady is the ghost of Christian Nimmo, wife of Andrew Nimmo, a city merchant. Her lover, Lord James Forrester, was already married to the daughter of General Patrick Ruthven (1573-1651).

Lord Forrester was fond of his ale and was often drunk. In one of his drunken moods he publicly criticised Christian. She sent her maid to tell him to meet in their usual place, the old sycamore tree near the dovecot in Corstorphine. Forrester came, drunk as ever, and spoke roughly to her. He told her to her face that he refused to marry her, as he had often refused before. In a desperate fury Christian pulled out Forrester's sword and ran him through the body. He died instantly. She left him in a pool of blood and hid in Corstorphine Castle.

She was discovered and sentenced to death, having confessed to the murder. She tried to avoid her punishment by petitioning the Privy Council (unsuccessfully), claiming that she was pregnant by Lord Forrester, and by escaping dressed in men's clothes. But she was caught in the Fala

Hills and locked up in the Tolbooth. On 12th November 1679 she appeared on the scaffold dressed in the mourning clothes of the time—pure white. She laid her head on the block and was beheaded.

An UNEXPECTED VISITOR

In 1689 Lord Balcarres was imprisoned in Edinburgh Castle for his Jacobite views. He was lying in his four-poster bed with the curtains pulled, when an unexpected visitor appeared. The curtains opened and he saw his great friend Graham of Claverhouse, 'Bonnie Dundee.' There was no sound—Claverhouse merely looked at him without a word. He moved and then disappeared. Some time later Lord Balcarres received news of the Battle of Killiekrankie (27th July 1689) at which his friend Claverhouse had been killed.

The GREEN LADY

Dating from the 1560s, the Old Craighouse is said to be haunted during a full moon by the ghost of Marie Carmichael (one of the famous 'Four Maries'), sorrowing for her two sons who tried to avenge the murder of her husband, Stephen Bruntfield in 1569 —with tragic results. During her life she shut herself up in an apartment hung with black cloth, lit by flickering candlelight.

❖

But in the eighteenth century, this unfortunate house held another terrible secret: it was haunted by the figure of the Green Lady.

Sir Thomas Elphinstone, a former governor of Maryland, had decided to marry a girl forty years younger than himself. Miss Betty Pettendale was herself in love with a dashing young officer whom she knew only as 'Captain Jack Courage,' a nickname he had acquired by his exploits with Marlborough in the French Wars. They had declared their love for each other, but he had been unable to marry her until his father died and left him the ancestral home. In the meantime he was recalled to Ireland with his regiment.

Betty became Lady Elphinstone, mainly due to the ambition of her parents. Four months later the old man was awaiting the return of his son from military service bearing the rank of colonel. Lord Elphinstone arranged a lavish reception to introduce his wife into society. He appeared to the company with his young bride and introduced her to his son. At once Betty knew him. It was her sweetheart who was now revealed as the young Colonel Elphinstone.

Colonel Elphinstone decided to go away for ever. At their last meeting in the year 1712 he said goodbye to Betty and gave her one last kiss. At that moment his father came into the room and stabbed his wife to death. Later that night he himself died over her dead body, consumed with remorse. Husband and wife were buried together.

Then the appearances began, to one person, then another. The Green Lady put fear into the hearts of many in the house, until an Eastern mystic was brought in to solve the mystery. He succeeded in raising the forms of Lord and Lady Elphinstone. The Green Lady asked that her body should be moved away from her husband, so that she could be near Colonel Elphinstone's when he came to be buried. This was done, and the Green Lady appeared no more.

WITCHCRAFT

Finally, the city of Edinburgh has a harsh reputation for its treatment of so-called witches over the centuries. There are those who believe that witchcraft is the old pagan religions gone underground after the coming of Christianity; there are others who see it as the product of the Counter-Reformation at a time when heretics had been tortured and burned and the people of Europe had acquired a taste for execution. Yet others see it as the hysterical victimisation of eccentrics. Whatever the root cause, it is a historical fact that great numbers of persons were put to death for being witches.

Between 1479 and 1722 more than 300 women were burned on Edinburgh's Castle Hill, and in Scotland more than 17,000 were tortured and executed for witchcraft. King James VI himself was a believer in witchcraft and he contributed to popular hysteria in 1597, publishing a treatise called *Daemonologie*. Sweeping powers to deal with those suspected of being witches were acquired in 1661 by the Town Council of Edinburgh, and one of those caught in their net was the infamous Major Weir.

'ANGELICAL THOMAS'

Major THOMAS WEIR (1600-1670) was born in Carluke and saw active service with Montrose's Covenanters in Ireland before being appointed a captain in the Edinburgh Town Guard. He was 'a tall black man, and ordinarily looked down to the ground,' Robert Chambers tells us. He hardly ever smiled, wore a dark cloak and lived in a tall dark house in the West Bow. He memorised and quoted many passages from Scripture, had great dignity and a gift for extempore prayer. He was above all a leading member of a puritanical offshoot of the Presbyterians known as the 'Bowhead Saints.'

In 1670 Weir suddenly confessed that he had committed incest with his sister Jane (by then aged 50) from when she was 16 years old. He also accused himself of bestiality with mares and cows and of witchcraft. 'Angelical Thomas,' as he was popularly known, stirred up a hornet's nest of hysteria and persecution. Stories were told about his walking-stick—it was carved with heads like satyrs and was reputed to carry messages for him, answer the door and act as a link-boy (torch-bearer) at night. Weir, who is now generally thought to have suffered from mental illness, was executed at the Gallow Lee in the Grassmarket.

The legends lingered: Thomas Chalmers wrote in the early 1800s, 'His apparition was frequently seen at night, flitting, like a black and silent shadow, about the street. His house, though known to be deserted by every human, was sometimes observed at midnight to be full of lights, and heard to emit strange sounds as of dancing, howling, and what is strangest of all, spinning .... '

Strange happenings indeed!

MAJOR WEIR'S LAND *in* 1830

PHILOSOPHY

The SCEPTIC

DAVID HUME (1711-76) was the greatest
of Scotland's philosophers. Born in Edinburgh, he was only two years of age when
his father died and so young David was
brought up by his mother.

Largely self-educated, he attended
Edinburgh University, but left without
graduating. Although intended for the
legal profession, at 18 he decided to make
philosophy his career and eventually moved
to London in 1734. From there he went to
France where he stayed for three years to
write the manuscript of his first and greatest work, the *Treatise of Human Nature.*

The *Treatise* was an attempt to introduce
the experimental method of reasoning into
moral subjects. Hume's conclusions made
him unpopular with many sections of the
Church of his time: the *Treatise* marks the
high point of scepticism—Hume argued
that we cannot trust our senses, our memory
or our imagination. Everyone who reasons
or believes in anything is a fool.

Hume tried twice to become a professor:
once in 1744 at Edinburgh and again in
1751 at Glasgow. He was unsuccessful on
both occasions. He travelled to Canada as

Advocate-General of all the forces under General St Clair (a distant relative) and as Secretary of St Clair's military embassy to Vienna and Turin in 1748-49.

Finally, in 1752, he secured the status he desired through his appointment as Keeper of Edinburgh's Advocates' Library. By this time, he was boasting that he could 'cover the floor of a large room with Books and Pamphlets wrote against him.'

In 1763, during an embassy to Paris, Hume fell under the spell of one Madame de Boufflers, a former mistress of a royal prince. Hume is said to have declared his love to her with considerable ardour.

During this period he also made friends with the French philosopher Rousseau, whom he received in England three years later and found to be decidedly neurotic.

Hume was appointed Under Secretary of State for the Northern Department, but after eleven months returned to Edinburgh where he died in what was ironically named St David's Street, after the greatest sceptic of them all! Notorious for his want of religious conviction—or at any rate for his attacks on revealed religion—he died a source of disappointment to certain clergymen who hoped for a deathbed conversion. David Hume met his end with tranquillity and without their ministrations.

An interesting tale surrounds his burial in the Old Calton burial ground. Groundless rumours that Hume had made a pact with the Devil led his many friends to keep a constant lamplit watch over the tomb for the first eight nights after the funeral, firing pistols into the air at intervals.

The ECONOMIST

ADAM SMITH (1723-1790), a native of Kirkcaldy in Fife, was the founder of the classical school of economics. He first rose to fame, while Professor of Moral Philosophy at Glasgow University, with his *Theory of Moral Sentiments* (1759). He had lectured at Edinburgh University on rhetoric and *belles lettres*, and remained a frequent visitor to the city. His most influential work, *The Wealth of Nations* (1776), put forward the theory of the division of labour, emphasising the fact that value arises from the labour used in production. He believed that in a *laissez-faire* economy, self-interest could coincide with the public good.

ADAM SMITH

'Jupiter' Carlyle records of Smith that 'though perhaps only second to [David Hume] in learning and ingenuity, [he] was far inferior to him in conversational talents.' Readers may take heart that Thomas Carlyle, although an admirer of the *Theory of Moral Sentiments*, considered *The Wealth of*

Nations, 'tedious and full of repetition.'

Adam Smith is buried in the Canongate kirkyard.

The SOCIOLOGIST

ADAM FERGUSON (1723-1816) was born in Perthshire and educated at Perth Grammar School and St Andrews University, after service as a chaplain with the Black Watch. He succeeded David Hume as Librarian of the Advocates' Library in 1757, resigning two years later to become Professor of Natural Philosophy, and then Moral Philosophy, at Edinburgh University. This demonstrated the brilliance and diversity of his intelligence which was remarked upon by his contemporaries.

ADAM FERGUSON

With his *Essay on Civil Society* (1766), which ran into several editions and was translated into most European languages, Fergusson may be said to have founded the modern discipline of sociology.

Cockburn paints the following picture of him: 'Our neighbour on the east was old Adam Ferguson ... when I first knew him, he was a spectacle well worth beholding. His hair was silky and white; his eyes animate and light blue; his cheeks sprinkled with broken red, like autumnal apples

… his lips thin, and the under one curled. A severe paralytic attack had reduced his animal vitality, though it left no external appearance, and he required considerable artificial heat. His raiment, therefore, consisted of half boots lined with fur, cloth breeches, a long cloth waistcoat with capacious pockets, a single-breasted coat, a cloth greatcoat also lined with fur, and a felt hat commonly tied by a ribbon below the chin ....'

RELIGION

The capacity for worship is second nature in Edinburgh. From the mists of prehistory, the standing stones—the Caiystane, the Catstane, the Camus stone—to the slender spires of the Christian churches, the city acknowledges, however fitfully, the existence of something beyond imagination.

A REFORMED MAN

JOHN KNOX (*circa* 1505-72) was born near Haddington in East Lothian and went on to study, it is believed, either at Glasgow or at St Andrews University. He was ordained a priest and was a papal notary in Haddington from 1540 to 1543. The following year he worked as a tutor to the sons of the lairds of Ormiston and Longniddry, East Lothian, who favoured the reformed religion.

By this time Knox had substantially rejected Roman Catholicism, particularly after the martyrdom of the reformer Patrick Hamilton in 1528. And when noted reformer

George Wishart returned to preach in Scotland and arrived in East Lothian in 1545, Knox became his companion, guarding him with a two-handed sword while he preached. When Wishart was himself executed in 1546, Knox became even more committed to reform, and because England had already gone down that road, he identified himself with anti-Papal England.

In 1546 Cardinal David Beaton, Archbishop of St Andrews, was assassinated. His executioners took over St Andrews Castle and made it a Protestant stronghold. Knox arrived there the following year with his pupils and began work as a Reformed minister. When the castle surrendered to the French some weeks later, Knox was made a galley-slave. Two years later, at Edward VI's request, he was released and he began to take a very active part in the English Reformation.

Knox was a minister at Berwick, at Newcastle-upon-Tyne and in London. He was appointed a Royal Chaplain and offered the bishopric of Rochester, but declined it.

During the reign of the Catholic Queen Mary of England, Knox was on the Continent—he was minister to the English exiles in Frankfurt, and in Geneva he ministered to the radical reformers who were opposed to the English settlement. There he met Calvin, whose theology and Church order he approved of greatly.

It was in 1559 that Knox was finally recalled from his self-imposed exile on the Continent. By 1560 the Estates (Scottish Parliament) had decided on religious reform. Knox and five assistants prepared the *Confession of Faith* which was approved by the Estates. It repudiated Papal jurisdiction and forbade the celebration of Mass.

Next came Knox's *Book of Discipline* (1560) which outlined a non-episcopal church constitution, a national plan for universal education from parish school to university, and a systematic programme of poor relief, all of these to be financed from the revenue received by the Kirk. In the same year the General Assembly of the Church of Scotland first met, and four years later the *Book of Common Order* which regulated the forms of public worship appeared. Knox was appointed minister of St Giles, Edinburgh, an office he held until his death.

When Mary, Queen of Scots returned to Scotland in 1561, she immediately celebrated Mass. Knox had already made clear his views on women rulers of nations in his *First Blast of the Trumpet against the Monstrous Regiment* [Government] *of Women*, a publication for which Queen Elizabeth I never quite forgave him. However, Knox returned to England in 1566 where he wrote his *History of the Reformation in Scotland*.

In 1572 he was back in Edinburgh, preaching for the last time in St Giles. He died shortly afterwards. Regent Morton's epitaph on Knox was: 'Here lies one who neither flattered nor feared any flesh.' Knox, who liked to compare himself to the Old Testament prophets, Amos and Jeremiah, saw himself very much in their mould, bringing a call to repentance from country pastures to the decadent cities. He has left the stamp of his character upon the Scottish nation, its Kirk and its system of education, which bear the imprint of his sense of purpose and moral integrity.

John Knox is buried in the precinct of St Giles.

The COVENANTERS

In Greyfriars churchyard stands the MARTYRS MONUMENT, erected in 1683 to the Covenanters who gave their lives in the Capital and all over Scotland. The Covenanters were originally so called because in 1638 they accepted the National Covenant, written at the Tailors' Hall in Edinburgh's Cowgate. The Covenant was later signed in Greyfriars kirk to demonstrate widespread opposition to Charles I's anglicisation of worship and the introduction of bishops into the Scottish presbyterian system.

When the General Assembly was convened in the then peaceful small town of Glasgow, away from the mobs of Edinburgh, the members condemned the King's new

prayer book and ruled that he had no power
to control the Kirk. The office of bishop
was abolished. The Covenanters began to
raise an army with the support of the most
powerful man in Scotland, the Earl of
Argyll. Among the Covenanter generals
was Alexander Leslie who had spent most
of his life abroad as a mercenary and had
risen to Field-Marshall in the Swedish army.
The Covenanters seized Edinburgh, Stirling
and Dumbarton castles. The ladies of
Edinburgh helped to carry earth and stones
to fortify the defences of the port of Leith,
and General Leslie and his army stood ready
on Leith sands: but a truce with the King's
army was eventually signed.

Charles I had his own battle with
Parliament in England—both sides wanted
the Covenanters to join them. However, in
1643 the Covenanters eventually drew up a
Solemn League and Covenant with the
English Parliament. The latter promised to
make the English Church presbyterian.
This promise did not materialise, but at a
conference in the Palace of Westminster the
Scottish Kirk accepted what is known as
the Westminster Confession, which, after
the Bible, was the cornerstone of the Church
of Scotland.

The Covenanters dominated Scotland
for eleven years, and the Kirk grew more
powerful than ever. Religion became
increasingly important, although in a nar-

row exclusive sense, for those who were not
for the puritanical regime were considered
to be beyond Redemption.

With the accession of Charles II in 1622,
bishops were one again introduced into the
Kirk. The Covenanters were forced to meet
secretly in conventicles in private houses or
in the hills, watching for the approach of
the dragoons. At Rullion Green in 1666,
the Covenanter army was defeated by
General Tam Dalyell, and thirty of them
hanged in Edinburgh.

By the 1680s—known as 'the Killing
Times'—there were few Covenanters left.
Those who were apprehended were taken to
Edinburgh to stand trial before 'Bluidy
Mackenzie' (Sir George Mackenzie, the Lord
Advocate). Those who were not sent to the
West Indies were hanged. Many were very
courageous, singing psalms or preaching a
sermon to the crowd. The Covenanters call-
ed this 'glorifying God in the Grassmarket,'
and the spot where they died is still marked
with a circle of stones and an inscription.

A MAN *of* LETTERS

ALEXANDER ('JUPITER') CARLYLE was born
in Prestonpans in 1722. He studied in
Glasgow and Leiden and was chosen as
minister of Inveresk, where he remained for
57 years, from 1748 to his death in 1805.
Carlyle was the friend of many men of let-

ters such as David Hume, Tobias Smollett and Adam Smith.

He copied out the manuscript of the play, *Douglas*, written by his contemporary, the minister John Home. Carlyle was censured by the more extreme clergy for attending the third night of the drama, for 'keeping company with an actress' and for 'taking possession of a box in an unlicensed theatre.'

Nevertheless, in 1770 Carlyle became Moderator of the General Assembly as leader of the 'Broad Church' party.

In 1789 he was made Dean of the Chapel Royal. His first and only large scale literary work (he published political pamphlets in the years 1758 to 1764) was his *Autobiography* (1860), which gives an invaluable picture of eighteenth century Scottish life and of Edinburgh society in particular.

The PLAYWRIGHT

JOHN HOME (1722-1808), the author of *Douglas*, was born in Leith, son of the town clerk. He attended Edinburgh University, and at the time of the 1745 Rebellion enlisted in the First (or College) Company led by Lord Provost George Drummond. Captured at the Battle of Falkirk, he was imprisoned in Doune Castle, but made his escape with a rope of bedsheets, breaking a leg in the process.

Home had a notion to be a dramatic poet. He went to London in 1749 with his *Tragedy of Agis*, but the actor-manager David Garrick thought it would not work on the stage.

From hearing an old ballad, Home worked up the theme of his next and most famous play, *Douglas*. Carlyle copied the manuscript several times and in 1755 it was completed for the stage, much to the admiration of the philosopher Hume, who thought it 'a Perfect Tragedy.'

JOHN HOME

Home set off for London, 'the Tragedy in one Pocket of his Great Coat, and his Clean Shirt and nightcap in the other,' as Carlyle observed. But again Home's work was rejected by Garrick, so the author returned to Edinburgh and persuaded the actor West Digges to put it on in the city.

The play (based on the agony of a mother whose son is killed by her husband) was stoutly patriotic, but aroused strong condemnation from that part of the clergy which frowned on the theatre. Its first performance proved a triumph, and the famous cry, 'Whaur's yer Wullie Shakespeare noo?' was shouted from the audience. The play went into twelve editions or more by 1800, and there were around twenty more during the nineteenth century.

Douglas was performed in 1757 in London, and indeed Home latterly became so friendly with the initially unimpressed Garrick that he was twice chosen as his second in two unfought duels. Garrick often invited Home to his house for dinner and later received a lesson in golf from the playwright, who was proficient at that sport.

John Home wrote four other plays, but none had the success of *Douglas*. He also wrote a *History of the Rebellion of 1745* which relates his personal experiences, and he spent his final years in Edinburgh. He was buried in St Mary's church, South Leith.

The CONVERT

GEORGE HAY (1729-1811) was born in the city, the son of a solicitor. His family were strong Jacobites and Episcopalians. Apprenticed to a surgeon at the age of 16, along with other Edinburgh doctors and medical students, he was required to treat the wounded at the Battle of Prestonpans (1745), when Prince Charles Edward Stuart's army defeated the Government's forces under General Cope. Hay went with the Jacobites into England, but took sick and was sent back to Scotland. After the Battle of Culloden, he was imprisoned in Edinburgh Castle and later in London.

In 1747 he was released and returned to Edinburgh. During his imprisonment in London, he met a Roman Catholic man, and after his release he took instruction in the Catholic faith and in 1748 became a convert.

He continued to study medicine, but was unable to graduate from the University because of the restrictions imposed on Roman Catholics by the Penal Laws.

Hay went to the Scots College in Rome in 1751 to train for the priesthood, was ordained in 1759, and was soon back in Scotland, where he was sent to Preshome to assist Bishop Grant. He was given a pony and rode out into the countryside, using his medical skill on Catholics and Protestants alike. He often travelled to Edinburgh on business for the Bishop. At his home in Edinburgh he rose very early to pray, ate very little but vegetables, and drank milk or water. His clothes were poor but clean, and he slept on a mattress with two blankets and no sheets.

In 1767 he was posted permanently to Edinburgh to minister to the Catholics in the city, large numbers of whom were evicted Highlanders. He worked as an agent for the Catholic Mission in Scotland, and in this capacity liaised between missionaries in Scotland and the seminaries abroad. In 1769 he was appointed a bishop and consecrated by Bishop Grant.

Part of Bishop Hay's new work was to assist Catholics who had been evicted from South Uist to emigrate to Canada. He also helped to re-establish the Scots College in

Madrid. Bishop Hay next travelled to Rome
to organise the running of the Scots College
there. His return journey was through
snow, hail and rain, and he was forced to
walk most of the way from Italy to Paris.

Back in Scotland Hay moved his head-
quarters to Aberdeen, still walking those
enormous distances, ' … striding along …
wrapped in a Highland plaid with a Highland boy behind carrying a knapsack.'

Hay opened two chapels in Edinburgh,
one in Blackfriars Wynd and another in
Leith Wynd. And he played a leading part
in the unsuccessful attempt in 1778 to
have the Penal Laws repealed. This aroused
the antagonism of those who were opposed
to Catholicism, and the Bishop had the
unpleasant experience of having to stand
watching at the roadside while his house
was looted.

Bishop Hay eventually retired to the
new seminary he had opened for 30 boys, in
Aquhorties near Inverurie. He had by now
written three works on Christian doctrine
and a two-volume treatise on miracles as
well as a number of pamphlets.

By 1800 there were 30,000 Catholics
in Scotland, ministered to by forty priests,
with twelve chapels.

Even as an old man, Bishop Hay made
several journeys to Edinburgh on horse-
back. He was an expert horseman as well
as a sturdy walker. He loved music, despite

his reputation for severity (which mellowed in old age). He died at 83, dreaming perhaps of the adventures he loved to describe of his early days following the Jacobite army.

The FOUNDER *of the* FREE KIRK

THOMAS CHALMERS (1780-1847) was born in Anstruther, Fife, the son of a dyer, ship-owner and general merchant. At the age of twelve he entered St Andrews University. Although he is said to have declared at the age of 3 that he intended to be a minister, and often gave sermons in his childhood, at university he at first appeared to be more interested in football and handball than his studies.

All that changed in his third year when Chalmers became enthused about mathematics and in 1795 began serious studies for the ministry (although his heart was reckoned to be in maths and chemistry). He was licensed to preach at 19 and delivered his first public sermon in Wigan in 1799, returning to Scotland to read chemistry, natural philosophy and moral philosophy at Edinburgh University. In 1803 he went to St Andrews University as assistant to one of the professors and taught mathematics.

He was ordained a minister at Kilmany and proceeded to open his own extra-mural classes in mathematics and chemistry at St

Andrews. He was appointed in 1823 to the Chair of Moral Philosophy at St Andrews and in 1828 to the Chair of Divinity at Edinburgh.

In the following year he actively campaigned for the emancipation of Roman Catholics and helped to set up Catholic schools. Other academic honours soon followed—for example, he was made Fellow of the Royal Society of Edinburgh in 1834 and a Doctor of Civil Law at Oxford.

The vexed question of church patronage, whereby a local laird had the right to impose a minister on a congregation against their wishes, came to a head when Robert Young was presented as minister to the church at Auchterarder by his lay patron, and was almost unanimously rejected by the congregation. Young appealed to the Court of Session, which ruled that a lay patron had the right to present regardless of the wishes of the congregation. This ruling, in the eyes of many, interfered with the right of the Kirk to govern its own affairs, and Chalmers, believing strongly in the principle of a church separate from the state, left the established Church of Scotland in 1843 with 470 ministers (out of about 1200) in what has come to be known as the Disruption. Out of this brave gesture grew the Free Church, and it was to be 1929 before a majority of its members reunited with the Church of Scotland.

Chalmers himself ministered to the poor in Edinburgh's West Port, believing that private Christian charity, and not state intervention, was the answer to poverty. He became in 1845 the first Principal of the new Free Church College, and died two years later.

Thomas Chalmers is remembered best for his principles, his magnificent oratory, his amazing energy and powers of organisation in so swiftly and successfully founding the Free Church. He is buried in the Grange cemetery, Beaufort Road.

Revd Dr THOMAS CHALMERS

The SOCIAL WORKER

Dr THOMAS GUTHRIE (1803-1872) was a native of Brechin. He graduated from Edinburgh University and was licensed to preach in 1825. He studied extra-murally with Dr Knox (the infamous anatomist), taking classes in Surgery and Anatomy, before continuing his medical studies at the University of Paris.

In Paris he saw vice and degradation which left a permanent impression on him. He returned to Edinburgh and worked in a bank before going to Forfar as a parish minister. Guthrie, like Dr Chalmers, was a firm opponent of the patronage system.

Moving to Old Greyfriars church in

Edinburgh's Cowgate, he was immediately
aware of the human suffering there.
In 1840 he opened a new church,
St John's, and at the time of the
Disruption was one of the leaders of the new Free Church.
His next church was Free St
John's in the West Bow, and it
was from there that he launch-
ed his appeal for a Ragged School
System to cope with the hundreds of
destitute children who roamed the streets
of the city. He proposed to offer education,
clothing and industrial training.

Revd Dr
THOMAS
GUTHRIE

The response of his congregation was
disappointing so he appealed to the general
public in 1847 in his *Plea for Ragged Schools*.
This pamphlet was favourably reviewed by
Hugh Miller and led to a meeting with the
then Lord Provost, Adam Black, and the
drawing up of a constitution and rules for
the new Society at a public meeting in the
Music Hall in George Street. Two more
Pleas followed, in 1849 and 1860.

As early as 1847 three schools had been
established with a total of 265 children. By
1851, some 216 young people trained by
the schools were recorded as having found
secure employment. The Governor of the
Calton Jail revealed that the number of
persons under the age of 14 in prison had
fallen from 5% of the prison population in
1847 to less than 1% in 1851.

Through the efforts of Dr Guthrie, after many vicissitudes, the Government passed a new Industrial School Act in 1866 which established the schools on a sound financial footing.

Dr Guthrie was a strong supporter of total abstinence and Sunday closing, as well as the strict control of the sale of liquor, derived from his observations of the effect of alcohol on the labouring poor. He travelled abroad to Switzerland (preaching in Geneva), Brittany and Belgium. He supported the Waldensian Church and was made Moderator of the Free Church in 1862. Like Dr Chalmers, Thomas Guthrie is buried in the Grange cemetery.

The FATHER of EPISCOPACY

Edinburgh-born ALEXANDER FORBES (1817-1875) was the son of a Scottish judge. He was educated at Edinburgh Academy and at the University of Glasgow.

He began his working life with the East India Company, but poor health forced him to return to Britain, and he decided to study for Holy Orders at Oxford. His first curacy was in Oxford, but he came back to Scotland in 1846 as rector of the Episcopal church at Stonehaven.

He returned to England, to the Anglo-Catholic church of St Saviour's in Leeds, but in 1847 was recommended by William

Gladstone and elected Bishop of Brechin. As a result of his work there, he became known as the father-figure of Episcopacy in Dundee and throughout Scotland.

Bishop Forbes introduced greater ritual and symbolism into Episcopal services along the lines favoured by the Oxford Movement, which stressed the closeness of the Episcopal Church to the Roman Catholic Church. This change was not achieved without opposition, as there were many who felt the Episcopal Church should be closer to traditional Protestant simplicity.

The DEAN of ST JOHN'S

Dean EDWARD RAMSAY (1793-1872) of St John's Episcopal church in Princes Street, was one of a select few who have had a memorial erected to them by public subscription. The monument, which stands at the West End beside St John's, takes the form of an imposing Celtic cross. His book *Reminiscences of Scottish Life and Character* was a humourous *tour de force* and ran to some 22 editions. He founded the Church Society and contrived to raise funds to send needy pupils to Trinity College, Glen-almond in Perth, an institution which he helped to found.

Dean Ramsay was the friend of many of the greatest men of his time—William Gladstone, Dean Stanley (the Archbishop

of Canterbury), the Duke of Buccleuch and
the Revd Dr Thomas Chalmers. He was a
respected philanthropist and also a keen
musician and flute-player. He lectured on
his favourite composer Handel and was
reputed to have the best church choir in
the city.

He was also an authority on bell-ringing,
church architecture and voice training (he
advocated the use of three pebbles in the
mouth to improve elocution). He was a
master of finance and responsible for raising
public interest and capital to erect a monument to Dr Thomas Chalmers. Dean
Ramsay presided at St John's for 44 years
and is buried there.

'The EDINBURGH WONDER WORKER'

MARGARET SINCLAIR (1900-1925) was
born in the basement flat of a dilapidated
tenement, the third child of a dustman.
Educated at St Anne's School in the Cowgate, she took certificates in sewing, cooking
and dressmaking at the Atholl Crescent
School of Domestic Economy, working
part-time as a messenger for a business firm
to support the younger children in the family. She then worked full-time as a french
polisher in the Waverley Cabinet Works
and became an active member of her trade
union. In 1918 the Cabinet Works closed

down and she was made redundant, but found other employment in McVitie's biscuit factory.

Joining the Order of Poor Clares, she spent two years at a convent in Nottinghill in London, before her untimely death from tuberculosis.

Over the years, many cures and apparent miracles have been reported as resulting from prayers to Margaret Sinclair. She was, during her life, a kind and caring, selfless woman who became known as the 'Edinburgh Wonder Worker.'

MARGARET
SINCLAIR

Cardinal Gordon Joseph Gray said of her that she 'may well be one of the first to achieve the title of Saint from the factory floor.'

Indeed she was declared Venerable by the Roman Catholic Church in 1978.

ROYALTY

MARGARET was born in Hungary and later
came to England. Thus, when William the
Conqueror landed in 1066, it was to Hungary that she, her mother and sisters and
Edgar, heir to the throne of England, tried
to escape. Margaret's ship, however, was
blown off course by storms and she landed
on Scottish soil instead, at Margaret's Hope
on the Firth of Forth, crossing over to
Queensferry.

Malcolm Canmore was King of Scotland
at that time. They met and, three years
after she arrived in Scotland, Margaret and
Malcolm were married. She was 24 years
old—he was almost twice her age.

Under her influence Scottish court life
became more civilised and English fashions
and customs were introduced to bring
Scotland into line with the rest of Europe
(while his Queen could read English and
Latin, for example, Malcolm himself was
illiterate).

She also tried to change the monastic
customs of the Scottish Culdee monks to
conform with the practices used by the
wider Christian community. And she
encouraged the installation of regular

diocesan bishops, regularised the date of Lent, Easter communion, marriage within the prohibited degrees and Sunday observance (she was shocked to find that Scots did manual labour on Sundays!)

In 1093 Malcolm was killed in an ambush at Alnwick. Three days later Margaret, who may have been anorexic, herself died in Edinburgh Castle.

For her work for the Church (such as rebuilding the Abbey at Iona), Margaret was canonised in 1251 and became officially known as 'Saint Margaret.'

The TRAGIC QUEEN

The fascinating **MARY, QUEEN of SCOTS** (1542-1587) did not have the statecraft of her mother, Mary of Guise, nor the acumen of her great rival, Queen Elizabeth I of England; yet the intrigues and contradictions of her life have made her the subject of art and literature. Her life was in many respects 'tragic'; in many respects 'romantic.'

MARY *of* GUISE, MOTHER *of* MARY, QUEEN *of* SCOTS

At 15, Mary married the Dauphin of France, soon to become King. Barely three years later, in 1561, now widowed, she landed at Leith. She arrived in a cold and hostile Scotland caught in the grip of Reformation: Mary was Catholic. In spite of her attractive personality, Mary's life after France was to become one ill-judged decision after another (both in her personal life and in affairs of state).

Mary married her weak contemptible cousin Henry, Lord Darnley (four years her junior), but the marriage was shortlived. Darnley was blown up as he lay, riddled with pox, in a house at Kirk o' Fields. Known to have despised him latterly, Mary was suspected of his murder. She then, too hastily, married the divorced Earl of Bothwell, also implicated in Darnley's murder. At a battle at Carberry, outside Edinburgh, the Scottish nobles, convinced of Mary's guilt, forced her to abdicate and imprisoned her in 1567 in Lochleven Castle.

MARY, QUEEN *of* SCOTS

DARNLEY *and* MARY'S CIPHER *in* EDINBURGH CASTLE

But Mary still had some allies. After her escape and subsequent defeat at Langside, she fled to England to seek the protection of Elizabeth I. Elizabeth found the presence of her rival, although in custody, increasingly dangerous as enemies of the Protestant Queen of England hatched plot after plot to restore Catholicism under Mary. Finally, a plot to assassinate Elizabeth was revealed and Mary's complicity was proved. In 1587 she was beheaded, dying with great dignity.

The SCOTS KING *of* ENGLAND

Mary's son, **JAMES VI of SCOTLAND** · succeeded Queen Elizabeth as James I of England in 1603, having, unlike his mother, proved an astute ruler of Scotland. Also, unlike Mary, he was a Protestant, and therefore—the enticements of English wealth apart—he could view England as a natural ally in the fight against the Catholic powers of Europe. He genuinely believed in the concept of 'Britain,' in which—as a man of considerable intellect—he was far ahead of the vast majority of his subjects, both English and Scottish.

However visionary this concept might have been, from Edinburgh's point of view it was disastrous. When James went off to England to rule his 'united kingdom,' the city lost an entire court as the Scottish nobles drifted down to London. There was a consequent impoverishment of life in Edinburgh, both cultural and material.

Scotland now began to enter England's orbit, a process which, in political terms, was completed in 1707 with the Union of Parliaments, leading to the end of the Scottish Parliament in Edinburgh. Ever since, Scottish Members of Parliament have travelled to Westminster.

Edinburgh, bereft of Court and Parliament, may be said to have the appearance instead of the substance of a Capital city, although it maintains a distinctive education and legal system, and a national church. But in spite of everything, Edinburgh is a thriving financial centre, reckoned second only to London in Europe.

The 'BONNIE' PRINCE

On 17th September 1745 **Prince CHARLES EDWARD STUART** (1720-88), intent on recapturing the lost Stuart throne from the House of Hanover, entered Edinburgh's King's Park at the head of his Jacobite army. Arriving at Holyrood Palace, he was welcomed by almost 20,000 people wild with enthusiasm for the heir of their ancient royal house.

CHARLES
EDWARD
STUART

A contemporary observed, 'He was in the prime of youth, tall and handsome, of a fair complexion; he had a light-coloured periwig, with his own hair combed over the front. He wore the Highland dress, that is, a tartan short coat without the plaid, crimson velvet breeches, and military boots; a blue bonnet was on his head, and on his breast the Star of the Order of St Andrew.'

Others observed that he looked melancholy, seeming more like a fashionable gentleman than a conquering hero. He was duly proclaimed King James VIII and

Charles Prince Regent at the Mercat Cross.

On the 19th, the Prince left Edinburgh for Duddingston (now part of Edinburgh) where he stayed the night in a cottage opposite the west entrance of Duddingston House, arranging for transport to be sent out from Edinburgh for the wounded in his impending battle for the throne.

The night before the Battle of Prestonpans the Prince slept in a field wrapped in his plaid. When dawn came he mounted a surprise attack on the Government forces, leaving only 170 alive and uncaptured out of 2000 captured or dead.

The Edinburgh surgeons tended the worst cases locally while the rest of the wounded (600 Government troops and 70 Highlanders) were taken to the Royal Infirmary and the Edinburgh Charity Work-house. Over 1000 prisoners were housed in the Canongate kirk and the Tolbooth, and most of the captured Highlanders came over to the Prince's side.

On the day after the battle the Jacobite army marched in triumph through the city, led by pipers playing the Prince's favourite tune, 'The King shall enjoy his own again.' The victorious clans came next, followed by the prisoners and wounded in carts at the rear. The Prince, meanwhile, was still at Prestonpans, supervising the care of the wounded. He spent the night at Pinkie House in Musselburgh, returning to the city of Edinburgh the following day.

The citizens of Edinburgh found the good manners of the Jacobite officers, and the discipline of the common soldier in the Prince's army, something of a surprise. During their occupation, there was no drunkenness or riots by the Highland army.

Not everyone was pro-Stuart, however. Provost George Drummond tactfully went to London to woo a wife; the poet Allan Ramsay retired with a diplomatic illness to Penicuik; the judges had already fled the city; and the two Edinburgh banks had sent all their cash and securities to Edinburgh Castle for safekeeping. The city clergy were given freedom to worship as usual.

By and large, however, Whigs and Jacobites co-existed peacefully. Edinburgh contributed passively to the Jacobite forces in the form of tents, military stores and arms, and the Jacobites, for their part, were content during the course of the seven weeks' occupation to go about their business in their distinctive Highland dress of white cockade, plaid waistcoat and Highland sash.

Later, after the Battle of Culloden and the defeat of the Rising, there was an Edinburgh mania for Jacobite tartan. Ladies wore it as plaids, gowns or riding habits, and made it into quilts, curtains, even shoes and pin cushions. Charles himself did not wear the kilt at any time in Edinburgh. His dress was either tartan trews or breeches.

And, contrary to the popular image of the Prince as a ladies man, he seemed quite distant in their company, and diffident, if not embarrassed. He preferred the military life to that of a fashionable gallant.

Charles did not succeed in capturing Edinburgh Castle, where 85 year old General Joshua Guest doggedly held out. The blockade of the city was eventually lifted and Charles departed for Dalkeith on 1st November. After the subsequent Battle of Culloden, rumours of a Jacobite victory were rife until the true outcome was known. The Stuart cause had ended.

'Edinburgh had not much cause to be proud of her conduct in 1745,' it has been observed. 'If she did little for King George II [the Hanoverian King], she did even less for Prince Charles.'

Charles died in Rome (his birthplace), his youthful good looks bloated and ravaged by disillusionment.

HOLYROOD & ARTHURS SEAT

SCIENCE
and
INVENTION

WIZARD
or MATHEMATICIAN?

JOHN NAPIER (1550-1617) was born at Merchiston Castle (now Napier University) in Edinburgh, where his father, the Master of the Scottish Mint, was Laird. The year of his birth marked the beginning of the Reformation in Scotland, and the young Napier was an early Protestant champion.

JOHN
NAPIER

Napier's education began in St Salvator's College at St Andrews University, and he is thought to have travelled extensively abroad (probably to the University of Paris, as well as visiting Italy and Germany). Upon his return to Scotland in 1571, an interest in theology acquired at university was broadened by research into literature and science.

By 1588 he was a commissioner to the General Assembly, representing the Presbytery of Edinburgh. In 1593 he published his *Plaine Discovery of the Whole Revelation of St John*, an attack on the Church of Rome. From that time, in preparation for an expected Spanish invasion, Napier was occupied with the invention of secret instruments of war. Like Leonardo da Vinci a century before, Napier designed a tank, a round metal chariot so constructed that its occupants could manoeuvre it rapidly while firing out through its small port-holes. He also invented a mirror to burn enemy ships at a distance; artillery for destroying everything within the arc of a circle; and a hydraulic screw for clearing water from coal mines.

Napier, at the same time, was a very successful landowner and farmer, making innovations in land use and artificial fertilisers. He also took a keen interest in alchemy, astrology, astronomy, magic and mathematics. In fact, his achievements in the latter were such that people could be forgiven for thinking there might be a touch of wizardry in him.

Napier took nearly 20 years to construct the table of logarithms for which he is best remembered. *Rabdologiae* (1617) was an account of ingenious methods of calculating, using 'rods' or 'bones.' Also described were methods of using little plates of metal in a box. Napier can therefore be considered as one of the early fathers of computer science.

John Napier died in 1617 and is buried in St Cuthbert's churchyard.

'*The* FATHER
of MODERN GEOLOGY'

JAMES HUTTON (1726-1797) was born

in Edinburgh, the son of a merchant, and educated at the High School. In 1743 he was apprenticed to a Writer to the Signet (solicitor) to follow a legal career. However, instead of copying legal documents as required, he often amused himself and his fellow apprentices by conducting chemical experiments. This passion for chemistry led him to study medicine at Edinburgh, Paris and Leiden, where he graduated MD in 1749. In the following year he returned to Edinburgh and, having been left a small property in Berwickshire by his father, his thoughts turned to agriculture. With a friend, James Davie, he set up a small business making salt from coal-soot.

JAMES
HUTTON

He then went to Norfolk to study rural economy and during his time there made many journeys on foot throughout England. He began to study mineralogy and geology, his mind fired by observations of the landscape. He also travelled through Flanders.

In 1785 Hutton read the outline of his famous *Theory of the Earth* to the Royal Society of Edinburgh. This work was to lay the foundations of modern geology by putting forward a 'plutonic' theory of the origin of earth—he pointed to heat as the principal agent in elevating land masses. This opposed the popular contemporary 'neptunean' theory which saw the sea as the main force in shaping the surface of the earth. Hutton lived in Edinburgh until his death and is buried in Greyfriars kirkyard.

The INVENTOR
of the STEAM-BLAST

JAMES NASMYTH (1808-1860) was a son of the Edinburgh artist Alexander Nasmyth. Alexander, as well as a talented painter, was a proficient engineer, designing mechanically powered boats with the entrepreneur banker Patrick Miller.

James attended the Royal High School from the age of nine to twelve, spending much of his leisure hours working at his father's lathe, making peeries (tops) and cannons for his schoolmates. He even set up a lathe in his bedroom with a small brass foundry and became expert in the casting of alloys.

From the age of 13 to 18 he studied at the Edinburgh School of Arts (the precursor of the present Heriot-Watt University) and he had the good fortune to meet the Glasgow-born inventor James Watt himself (by then an old man of 82).

JAMES
NASMYTH

James Nasmyth made a large number of models, mainly steam engines, which he sold to pay for his classes at Edinburgh University.

He visited as many local engineering

works as he could in order to sketch engines and other machinery. And at the age of 19 he designed and built a working model of a steam road-carriage which he exhibited to the Royal Scottish Society of Arts. It worked so well that he was subscribed £60 for building a full-scale version of his car, which he ran up and down the Queensferry Road carrying eight passengers. He could be regarded as a pioneer of the modern motor-car. Moreover, independently of George Stephenson, Nasmyth invented the steam-blast on which the locomotive came to be based.

In 1840 a paddle-shaft 36 inches in diameter was needed for Isambard Kingdom Brunel's steamship 'Great Britain,' and no forge could be found big enough to make it. Nasmyth designed the required steam-hammer in 20 minutes. But the ship's engines were subsequently changed from paddle to screw propulsion, and Nasmyth's steam-hammer was not actually constructed. Later, while visiting the renowned Creusot works in France, he was surprised to see an enormous crank forged with a steam-hammer. He was informed that this was indeed his design which had finally been built.

The steam-hammer piledriver was his next invention in 1854: then a planing machine, a nut-shaping machine, and a hydraulic punching machine. After he retired in 1856, he made his own telescopes and carried out a number of interesting astronomical observations.

James Nasmyth is buried in the Dean cemetery.

The TELEPHONE MAN

ALEXANDER GRAHAM BELL (1847-1922) was born at 16 South Charlotte Street and attended the Royal High School. He later left for London to study physiology and anatomy. There he was introduced to Sir Charles Wheatstone, a scientist working in the fields of electricity, telegraphy, cryptography, the physiology of vision, and the science of sound.

Upon Bell's return to Edinburgh, his father, a Professor of Elocution, challenged him and his brother to build a machine that could talk. This they did from a lamb's larynx, two sheets of rubber, a copy of human jaws, teeth, pharynx and nasal cavities moulded from a real skull. They added rubber lips and rubber cheeks, a soft palate made from rubber stuffed with cotton and made a tongue from wooden sections which could be raised or lowered. When this contraption was complete they blew into a metal tube to imitate the action of the lungs. After some practice the speaking head was able to say 'Mama' in such a convincing fashion that one of the neighbours on the stair wondered what could be the matter with the baby!

Bell began to assemble a range of skills, experience and research which would enable him to develop the telephone. He became an amateur telegrapher, and investigated the design of an electric piano operated by an electro-magnet, at the same time extending the range of application of his father's own system of Visible Speech.

In 1870 Bell's father, worried about his son's health (after the recent death of his older brother from tuberculosis), and anticipating new fields to conquer, per-suaded his son to accompany him to Canada. And it was Alexander Graham Bell's subsequent work, while Professor of Vocal Physiology at Boston University, which led to the invention of the telephone, which he patented in 1876.

STREET LIFE

SELLERS
of FOOD *and* DRINK

Of all Edinburgh's many legendary characters, it was the street vendors who were
the most numerous and most colourful. At
a time before the development of modern
large-scale distribution techniques, it was
the hardy street vendor striding from house
to house, or standing in the markets, who
provided the hundred and one necessities
and luxuries of city life.

The more mundane household goods or
repair services were supplied by wandering
tradesmen. A great number of them took
up their stances in the markets, or outside
important buildings, shouting their wares.
These included the cadies (carriers of water,
parcels and news, or town guides),
ballad-criers, travelling cobblers,
sellers of fruit and vegetables (the
kailwives) and fishwives, all of
them competing with their own
distinctive cries, loudest at night.
The traditional cries continued to
about 1870, but from that time
they began to disappear and, like
rare songbirds, were then heard no
more.

The
WATER
CADIE

From time immemorial the High Street of Edinburgh was full of noise and confusion as the street traders shouted their wares. The Luckenbooth shops and the Krames' open stalls both crammed against the north wall of the kirk of St Giles and filled up with people forcing their way through the mud and filth of the narrow arcade known as the 'Stinking Stile.' And there was always the danger of having a housewife's slops dropped on you from the houses above.

In the autumn the town was full of the calls of the apple sellers, one of the most famous being SARAH SIBBALD, known as 'Apple Glory.' She sat in Shakespeare Square outside the old Theatre Royal (where the Head Post Office now is). She had met many of the greatest names on the British stage and she talked about them with fierce pride.

The trade with the best-remembered cries was that of the fishwife. Everyone in Edinburgh last century knew the cries of 'Cockles an' Wulks,' 'Wulks an' Buckies' or 'Cockles an' Mussels.' Early each Spring, when the biting wind still blew off the Forth, women from Musselburgh, Newhaven, and even Dunbar down the east coast, trudged up the steep roads to the city and took up their stances in the Old Town.

In spite of the building of a spacious and prosperous New Town, the main stances of the vendors continued to be in the High Street. So the fishwives set up their stalls at the street corners, often on upturned wooden boxes, displaying the shellfish in little saucers along with salt, pepper and spoons. Children loved mussels better than sweets and were always seen at the roadside besieging the fisher-women.

The most haunting of the shellfish cries was that of 'Caller Oysters.' From September to April the oyster vendors came, often to the New Town, for it was mainly there that the popular oyster cellars were to be found. For much of the eighteenth century, oyster parties were all the rage as, the cellars being hidden from public view, an atmosphere of frivolity and abandon was generated— which most red-blooded citizens preferred to the staid decorum of the assemblies with their slow-moving dancing and old-fashioned gavottes.

The popular fishwives, who for a long time provided the city with crabs and herrings, were a hardy breed. MAGGIE DICKSON, for example, was hanged in 1724 for concealing the birth of a stillborn illegitimate child. The executioner allowed her to hang for the required time and even jerked her legs (as was the custom) to make sure no life was left. She was nailed into a coffin, and on her way to her burial at Inveresk her friends stopped to refresh themselves at an inn. On

The FISHWIFE

leaving the inn some time later, one of the company thought he heard a strange noise coming from the coffin. The lid was hurriedly prised open, a vein was bled and some spirits were poured down Maggie's throat. That evening she had recovered sufficiently to speak and was soon receiving financial contributions from all and sundry who came to marvel at her recovery. As she had been officially pronounced dead, she was allowed to go free. She was known thereafter as 'Half-hangit Maggie.' Maggie lived to a ripe old age as an innkeeper, dying finally in the arms of one of her many lovers.

The fishwives had the reputation of possessing the manners and the strength of men. Three of them are recorded in the *Old Statistical Account* as travelling barefoot the 27 miles from Dunbar to Edinburgh in the space of five hours, with loaded creels on their backs. They played golf before it was fashionable for women to do so, and on Shrove Tuesday the married fisherwomen played the spinsters at football, a game which the married ladies usually won. Three days after the birth of a baby, many of them would go out again with the creel.

The visitor to the Newhaven Inn often passed by the closes between the fisherfolk's houses. The reek of tan would be in the air. Floats, fishing-lines and oilskins hung on the stairs among the innumerable dark blue stockings of the women who sat baiting their lines and gossiping.

The working dress of the fishwives was a thick blue petticoat, a blouse and serge gown over it, and a blue apron with a white stripe. In bad weather a small head shawl was worn with a blue and white checked pattern. The creel itself was in two parts: in the lower larger half, the fresh fish was carried; in the top half, the 'skull,' knitting and other odds and ends were stored, or it could be used as a hand basket. Often the fisherwives carried as much as 250 lbs on their backs in their wickerwork creels.

On special occasions the Newhaven fisherwomen wore yellow and white, or red and white costumes and Paisley shawls. These costumes are said to have been the dress of the Flemish women whose husbands came to Newhaven in 1507 to build the warship 'The Great Michael' for James IV.

Some aspects of the fish trade, however, were far from romantic or colourful. Lord Cockburn tells us that 'our only fish market was in Fish Market Close, a steep, narrow stinking ravine. The fish were generally thrown out on the street at the head of the close, whence they were dragged down by dirty boys or dirtier women; and then sold unwashed ... from old rickety, scaly, wooden tables, exposed to all the rain, dust and filth; an abomination, the recollection of which greatly impaired the pleasantness of the fish at a later hour of the day.'

In the early 1800s, Lord Cockburn continues, 'our vegetables had to pass through as bad a process. They were entirely in the hands of a college of old gin-drinking women, who congregated with stools and tables round the Tron church. A few of the aristocracy of these ladies, the burgomistresses, who had established a superior business, the heads of old booths, marked their dignity by an awning of dirty canvas or tattered carpet; and every table had its tallow candle and paper lantern at night. There was no water here either, except what flowed down the gutter, which, however, was plentifully used. Fruit had a place on the table but kitchen vegetables lay bruised on the ground.'

The cabbage-seller best remembered in history was **JENNY GEDDES**, who worked in the High Street. When in 1623 Charles I tried to introduce English ways of worship into the churches of Scotland, he appointed a Bishop of Edinburgh and renamed the High Kirk of St Giles, 'St Giles Cathedral.' The new order of service and the new prayer book were to be introduced on a Sunday in July, but the majority of the people of Scotland strongly objected to the anglicisation of their liturgy.

When the prayer book was to be read for the first time in St Giles, many citizens crowded into the kirk. The Town Council was there; the magistrates, law lords and two bishops took their places in the large congregation. After the choir had stopped singing, the Dean, James Hanna, went up the pulpit steps, paused, opened the new prayer book, and a hush fell on the congregation as they listened to the first words ....

Then a voice bellowed, 'Are ye sayin' mass in ma lug?' Next moment a stool sailed through the air, narrowly missing the Dean's head. Pandemonium broke out, and the bishop was only just able to escape the furious mob. History credits Jenny Geddes as having thrown that first celebrated stool.

For residents who wanted food cooked in a hurry, the pudding and pie sellers did a roaring trade. They carried their wares in a charcoal grill over their shoulders and, in later years, displayed them in a stand by the roadside. Black puddings were as popular as white, and most people enjoyed the plain meal pudding. Soup was also available in the streets. In the eighteenth century a man carrying a leg of mutton walked the streets crying 'Twa dips an' a wallop for a bawbee.' This was the signal for the housewives to come to their door with pails of boiling water into which the leg of mutton was dipped, producing the basis of a good broth. Most people could not afford to buy cuts of meat, relying on offal—tripe, pigs' trotters or sheep's head—to fortify their diet. Vendors carried sheep's heads in baskets through the streets.

Long before the appearance of that modern delicacy, yoghurt, in Scotland, the people in Edinburgh were great customers of buttermilk ('soor-dook' as it was known). Every morning the milkmaids would ride into the High Street carrying soor-dook barrels strapped to the saddles of their horses. A favourite summer dish was curds. During June and July the vendors sat spooning white chunks of it into their customers' dishes to the cry of, 'Curds an' Whey, Curds an' Whey.'

Sweets, ice-cream, gingerbread and coconut were bought from street vendors such as **THOMAS SIMPSON**, known as 'Coconut Tam,' a little bent man dressed in black and wearing a bowler hat. His shrill cry was 'Cocky nit, cocky nit; a ha'penny the bit, bit, bit. Taste an' try afore ye buy, for that's the way tae make ye buy.' Simpson, with his thin-voiced cry, died in 1874 at the age of 71, and in recent years has had a public house named after him.

THOMAS SIMPSON *alias* 'COCONUT TAM'

But probably the most famous character associated with street commerce is **GREYFRIARS BOBBY**, the faithful police dog who refused to leave the graveside of his master, a constable, John Gray, who died in 1858 while policing a Wednesday market. Bobby stayed at his master's grave in Greyfriars cemetery for 14 years until he died. His statue in nearby George IV Bridge is now a regular port of call for guided tours and visiting photographers.

SELLERS *of* HARDWEAR *and* SERVICES

A vital piece of household equipment was the spit or roasting-jack. A grisly tale attaches to this everyday kitchen utensil. The 2nd Duke of Queensberry (one of the main architects of the 1707 Act of Union) had a mentally-handicapped son, who was enormously strong and very tall, but who was hidden away in a room with boarded up windows in Queensberry House in the Canongate. On the day of the signing of the Act of Union, the 'monster's' keeper went outside for a moment to watch the crowds in the street. Time passed, and when the Duke eventually returned home, he found to his horror that his son was sitting in the kitchen at the spit, roasting the kitchen-boy.

GREYFRIARS
BOBBY

One of the best known sellers of roasting-jacks was LAUGHLAN MCBAIN, a hardy veteran of Culloden. McBain manufactured his own jacks and toasting forks and advertised his wares with such a piercing voice as he paraded from the Cowgate to Parliament Square, that the judges and lawyers in the Courts could only persuade him to be quiet by collecting a sum of money large enough qute simply to buy his silence.

Tobacco first came to Edinburgh around 1560, and it spread like wildfire; so much so that the testy intellectual King James VI decided to depose the last vicar of Gullane for the abominable habit, and wrote a virulent *Counterblast to Tobacco*, linking the practice of smoking that drug with all kinds of unspeakable vices. Within a few years, however, tobacco was being indulged all over Scotland, and gentlemen in coffee houses up and down the Royal Mile smoked their long church-warden pipes, read the latest gazette from London and discussed the prices on the Exchange. Soon snuff caught on too, pinched on the back of the thumb, scented with oil of orange-blossom or burgundy wine.

The records of the City Chambers note a number of tobacco mills and tobacco shops. There were five mills at Colinton, and one at Canonmills, but **JAMES GILLESPIE** (1725-1797) at 231 High Street was probably the city's most famous snuff manufacturer, sub-

JAMES GILLESPIE'S SHOP SIGN

sequently famous as the founder of James Gillespie's School. Gillespie is buried at Colinton churchyard. His grinder remains in the city's possession; and also his shop sign—a black boy holding a clay pipe, dressed in green trunks, leaning on a barrel.

In the city's tobacco shops the precious commodity was stored in white jars imported from Holland. Juniper wood was kept burning in a dish, and the customer took a glowing ember with a pair of silver tongs to light his clay pipe.

Of all the places of commerce in the city it was the Krames, clustered around St Giles kirk, that fired the imagination and lived longest in the memory. Lord Cockburn wrote: 'In my boyhood their little stands, each enclosed in a tiny room of its own, and during the day all open to the little footpath that ran between the two rows of them, and all glittering with attractions, contained everything fascinating to childhood, but chiefly toys .... '

Fire was vital for heating and cooking, so the seller of spunks for ignition was sure of a crowd. A spunk was a stick six inches long, smeared with brimstone at both ends, which had to be brought into contact with flint, steel and tinder. In later years, the spunk-seller was replaced by the lucifer match-seller with his 'Here's your fine lucifer-matches, only a bawbee the box.' In the nineteenth century a number of match-sellers are recorded, such as SANDY MALCOLM, who had been blinded in an explosion in Noble's works at Falkirk in 1879. He sold matches at the Waverley Market railings.

The possibility of fire was, of course,

always a recurrent nightmare, especially in the Old Town with its overcrowding; in the old timber houses, crammed together, the smallest spark could and did lead to enormous devastation and loss of life.

To prevent this dreadful catastrophe a band of fire-fighters known as the Tronmen was formed. With their flat bonnets, knee-breeches, ladders and coils of rope, they provided an essential chimney-sweeping service. The Tronmen, under their Captain of the Chimneys, were often helped by the city's Street Overseers and their Muckmen (street-cleaners) who would convey loads of horse manure in creels (baskets) on their backs to the scene of a fire. Unloaded on the flames, the manure gave off fumes which acted as a chemical extinguisher.

After 1824, when a number of great fires had destroyed much of the High Street, the city set up its first fire brigade, the Edinburgh Fire Establishment, the first municipal brigade in Britain. The moving spirit behind this was JAMES BRAIDWOOD (1800-1861).

Communication in the city was of the utmost importance. In the seventeenth century, newspapers were cried in the streets by boys who also hawked flowers and acted as link-boys to light pedestrians going from one part of the city to another by night. In 1699 these lads had been required to enroll themselves into a society, which later became known as the Society of Running Stationers or Cadies, with a constitution drawn up by the magistrates.

Between 1667 and 1850 special open-fronted sedan chairs were introduced to cope with Edinburgh's uniquely narrow closes. The cadies who carried passengers waited at street corners, smoking, chewing or snuffing.

Around 1557 an order was issued that no one should go out into the city after dark without a lantern or torch or candle. The link-boys who provided this service were superseded in 1818 by gas lighting, and a number of shops and streets were also lit by gas jets. The 'leeries' who went from street to street lighting the gas lamps have been immortalised in R L Stevenson's poem 'The Lamplighter':

> My tea is nearly ready
> and the sun has left the sky;
> It's time to take the window
> to see Leerie going by;
> For every night at tea-time
> and before you take your seat,
> With lantern and with ladder
> he comes posting up the street.

(*A Child's Garden of Verses* 1896)

One of the best-known was LEERIE SMITH. Every day in times past there was the parade of the lamplighters in Hunter

Square, queuing up to receive their quota of oil and wicks to fill their 'crusies' and the 'flambeau' (a thin metal tube stuffed with tow and saturated with oil at the top). Then they would divide up and disperse to their allotted rounds through the streets of the city, with their cheerful and reassuring flame.

STREET MUSICIANS

Although fiddlers and singers were expelled from the streets of Edinburgh in 1587 by order of the Town Council, Edinburgh, like most ancient cities, has a long tradition of street entertainment carried on by those anonymous or forgotten figures whose dexterity and vocal exertions charmed, pacified or infuriated the passing crowds.

GEORGE CRANSTOUN *in his* CREEL

Out of the mists of anonymity step artistes like **DAVIE ARKLAY** and **JAMIE MAIN**, both blind, who sang for their suppers in the 1890s. And back in the eighteenth century, there was poor **GEORGE CRANSTOUN**, once a teacher of music, who was so small that when he was drunk (which was often) he was pushed into a creel and rolled home to his mother—until the day, that was, when the porter, balancing the creel precariously on the railings while he rang the door bell, looked round to see him crash to his death in the basement below.

And what about the 'Nightingale,' whose identity long remained shrouded in mystery? She sang in the New Town late at night, a dark veil draped over her face. It was rumoured that she had once been an opera singer, but she turned out to be KATE POWELL, a convent-educated teacher, fluent in four languages, who had begun her singing career after the death of her husband in 1890.

There was also blind WILLIE SANGSTER who sat on a stool playing his accordion; GEORGE PATERSON, who died in 1944, a fiddle-player and a favourite with the poorer children; the imposing figure of HERBERT PARKIN, with his ever-present cigar, bristling red beard, six raincoats and little spaniel (he had trained as a violinist with the Brighton Theatre Orchestra); blind JIMMY BROWN, who played the melodeon, and WILLIE MAXWELL who sang Robert Burns songs, accompanying himself on the accordion.

SHOWS *and* FAIRS

Like all medieval cities, Edinburgh was enlivened by seasonal frivolity. With its steep crags, its narrow, twisting walk-ways, it was a natural theatre, even latterly, in the broad panoramas of the New Town.

In medieval times, on the first morning in May, the townsfolk marched to the Burgh Muir to bring summer home—the procession tumbled along the High Street, a riot of drums, flags, cannons, guisers and dancers; and they returned in the same way, carrying birch branches high above their heads.

During December, the Abbot of Unreason presided at Holyroodhouse, and on New Year's day the King of the Bean ruled. In 1579 the ever-popular plays of Robin Hood were suppressed by order of the Provost and Baillies, and eight years later the Town Council expelled all minstrels, pipers, fiddlers and singers of profane songs from the city. Such rigour did not, fortunately, last; very soon the streets of the city and its environs became once again places of public entertainment.

Fairs were held regularly throughout the year—in July, for example, and at Hallowe'en. In the Grassmarket a weekly grain and livestock market was a great attraction for many decades. The Hallow Fair was held in the Grassmarket from the Bowfoot to the end of the West Port. Here the booths and barrows of the huxters were placed—the smell from scores of paraffin oil jets did not deter members of the general public from gorging themselves on gingerbread, sliced coconut and black pudding.

Ear-splitting music filled the air from the travelling booths with their human monstrosities, the menageries with their lion-tamers and the Punch and Judy man. One of the best-known showmen was **NED HOLT**. Originally apprenticed to a baker, Holt became an actor playing in the penny gaffs (laughs); he acted Hamlet in Connor's geggie (travelling theatre) off the High Street, rolling home drunk to his home in the White Horse Inn. He claimed to be able to kill rats with his teeth and, in his booth in the Grassmarket, he displayed the Fat Lady, the Living Skeleton and the Petrified Mummy. This last was supposed to be a thousand years old—it was encased in a roughly-made wooden box in the shape of a coffin with a glass top, and people paid a penny to view this 'Relic of the Pharaohs.' After many years Holt confessed that the relic was a fake—he had brought the skeleton for a few shillings and covered it with pliable india-rubber and bark from the West Port tannery.

One of the most violent entertainments in the city was the cockfight. Although banned from the streets in 1702, cock-fighting took place regularly in the cockpit at the Grassmarket from 1780; this was also the scene of meetings of the outlawed Jacobites and sympathisers with the French Revolution.

Less blood-thirsty excitement was to be

found at Leith Races. On race days a public holiday would be declared, with a procession from the Council Chambers to Leith carrying the City Purse decorated with ribbons, led by a file of the City Guard, bayonets fixed, a drummer beating them down Leith Walk. Once at Leith, people crowded among the tents and booths covered with canvas—recruiting-sergeants with drummers, sailors ashore, servant girls and apprentices. In and out of the drinking-places they went, and to the shows—the roley-poley, hobby-horses and wheels of fortune. Afterwards came the scrum as the crowds returned to the city up Leith Walk. In 1816 the races were transferred to Musselburgh.

STREET GAMES

Childhood games have always been an important part of the bustling, hectic life of the city. The nineteenth century scientist James Clerk Maxwell, wrote that he revelled in such games as bools and peeries. Bools were marbles made of clay, glass or steel. Peeries were tops, pear-shaped and whipped by a leather throng. A humming-top was called a French peerie. Diabolo or Diavolo (the Devil) was also a favourite of Clerk Maxwell, and he wrote in 1848 that he had played 'a game of the Devil of whom there is a duality and a quaternity of sticks [a pun on the River Styx] so that I can play either conjunctly or severally. I can jump over him and bring him round without leaving go the sticks. I can also keep him up behind me.'

Children's games in the city were not slow to reflect *every* aspect of life—below is a skipping song about the famous One o' Clock Gun, still fired daily from the castle:

One o' clock the gun went off—
I dare not stay no longer;
If I do, mother will say:
'Playing with the boys up yonder.'

Stockings red, garters blue,
Trimmed all round with silver;
A red red rose upon my head
And a gold ring on my finger.

Sometimes children in the street would play Mary Queen of Scots, chanting:

Mary Queen of Scots—
Got her head chopped off
Got her head chopped off
Got her head chopped off
Mary Queen of Scots—
Got her head chopped off
OFF!

Then they proceeded to chop the head off a dandelion flower, watching eagerly as the white gossamer floated away on the wind.

Another popular street game for many years was Peevers (Hopscotch). A pattern of chalked beds or boxes was marked out on the ground over which the peever was pushed by the hopping foot. Peevers would be made out of a round tin box, a piece of tile, a small marble chip, slate, wood or even glass. A glass peever can still be seen in Huntly House Museum in the Canongate.

Incidentally, Edinburgh is still a repository of children's games of the past and the present. This is mainly due to the efforts of the late **PATRICK MURRAY** (1908-81). Edinburgh-born and resident all his life, apart from his schooldays at Stonyhurst in Lancashire, he was an optician before his election to the Town Council. While he was chairman of Edinburgh Corporation's Libraries and Museums Committee he started the Museum of Childhood, first in Lady Stair's House in the Lawnmarket and, after 18 months, at a new site in the High Street at Hynford's Close. He began the collection with a number of his own toys, 'a pitiful handful of soldiers, building blocks and railway stuff of my own.'

The Museum was the first of its kind in the world, dealing not just with toys, but with the customs, hobbies, health, upbringing and education of children from birth to around the age of twelve. His idea has since been copied by many countries.

CONCLUSION

Edinburgh is a town of cliques and cabals, a mysterious and almost deserted medieval ramp; to the north an eighteenth century geometric wasteland, and, all around, the sprawl of suburban warrens. Across this abruptly-angled terrain scurry the inhabitants of the city, their paths crossing and re-crossing.

Edinburgh, like any other Capital city, has always been a magnet for talent and ambition or just plain curiosity. And, deep down, it welcomes the injection of new blood which the incomer and the tourist willingly brings.

Information on the final resting-places of many Edinburgh Characters can be found in *The Edinburgh Graveyard Guide*, Michael T R B Turnbull (Saint Andrew Press).

'MONS MEG' *at* EDINBURGH CASTLE

INDEX
of
CHARACTERS